SMOKE &
MIRRORS

The Illusion of the Employment Services Sector

Sarah Delicate and Angela Hoyt

ILLUSTRATED BY JON KLASSEN

 FriesenPress

One Printers Way
Altona, MB R0G 0B0
Canada

www.friesenpress.com

Illustrations by Jon Klassen

ISBN
978-1-03-911830-0 (Hardcover)
978-1-03-911829-4 (Paperback)
978-1-03-911831-7 (eBook)

1. *BUSINESS & ECONOMICS*

Distributed to the trade by The Ingram Book Company

CONTENTS

FOREWORD

W E STARTED THIS book four years ago, and the isolation brought by COVID-19 provided the opportunity to complete it. Over the past many months, we have asked ourselves many times whether we should publish it. We have talked each other into it and out of it, and into it again. We were afraid of losing relationships with our clients that, in some cases, have been over twenty years in the making. While we were often hired by these employment services sector clients to uncover the ugly truths and share the brutal facts about the way their programs were running, these facts were mostly shared in private so they could address issues proactively. Through our work and our research, however, we have come to understand that some of these ugly truths and brutal facts are systemic in nature and international in scope. We felt compelled, therefore, to write about it, and we expect some of our clients will still wonder (because we have been asked before): "Whose side are you on?"

We were concerned that by publishing this book now, still in the midst of a pandemic, we would be *kicking people when they are down*, especially those on the front line of the employment services sector. We considered postponing publication but then quickly realized there will always be some kind of major event that will knock us off our game: economic downfalls, environmental catastrophes, political strife, and, yes, pandemics. We concluded that the only time to deliver this message is now.

From a workforce perspective, COVID-19 has revealed the privileges of "white collar" workers, many of whom were given the opportunity to work from the safety of home, and the disparities between them and "pink collar" and "blue collar" workers, who have kept the economy running despite putting themselves at risk of infection. It has left people from disadvantaged groups who want to work but were not working prior to COVID-19 at a further disadvantage as they compete for fewer jobs against more qualified candidates. During COVID-19, the employment services contracted to help these groups were either closed or not accessible. The everyday challenges of unemployment for disadvantaged populations were made even more challenging with COVID-19. As lock-down restrictions lifted, some employment service centres were hesitant to reopen, a privilege only had by those with secure government funding.

We are optimistic that the shockwave of COVID-19 will provide an opportunity to set a new course for the employment services sector. But, we were optimistic after other major events. The observations we are sharing in this book did not start with COVID-19. They are not observations from an isolated incident, nor are they about any one organization, program, or community. They are patterns we have witnessed consistently over the past 30 years. People in our client organizations have come and gone, but the issues remain and, in some cases, have worsened.

We have learned from COVID-19 that big transformational change does not always happen incrementally; it sometimes happens all at once. If governments had told us we had five years to move a large part of the workforce to virtual services, it would have taken over ten years, or even on "the first day of never." We have been encouraging virtual service options for over a decade as part of a holistic customer experience and often heard it was impossible. Throw a pandemic into the mix and suddenly many companies and individuals adapted very quickly. Some highly resilient companies were nimble and did not miss a beat. Unfortunately, others are still wondering who turned the lights off.

Whose side are we on?

We are on the side of organizations that have to operate under the "ask for forgiveness, not permission" principle in order to deliver results; of practitioners who focus on doing the right thing, even if it costs them; and of individuals who went to employment centres looking for a job and received services that left them behind.

We are on the side of those who demand equity, diversity, and inclusion in workplaces and communities (as we all should).

What we know about readiness is that we are never fully ready and it is never the perfect time, so here we are.

Welcome to our book, *Smoke and Mirrors!* In this book, we aim to dispel the illusion that government-funded employment services lead to meaningful employment for disadvantaged groups unable to secure employment on their own. While the sector often hits the government-mandated performance targets, it usually misses the point— and the cost of the illusion is immense.

We would like to introduce you to "The Grand Illusionist," who is currently hiding in many offices in the employment services sector. He will accompany us on our journey.

Sarah Delicate and Angela Hoyt
March 2022

INTRODUCTION —
The problem defined

The problem defined

W E HAVE AN employment problem, and it is massive . . . like, globally massive.

Simply put, some people who *want* to work and *can* work, are not working. *Even if the jobs are there.*

Many of these people belong to groups that are under-represented in the labour market, such as Indigenous persons, persons with disabilities, NEET (Not in Employment, Education, or Training) youth, persons with a criminal history, women, racialized persons, immigrants, and refugees.

So, how is this a problem?

From a **government perspective**, people who are not working are not *contributing* to the economic fabric of society. There are no tax dollars being collected for health care, education, pensions, and so on. If unemployed people are not contributors to the system, then they are more likely to be dependent on the system. They depend on government financial aids and programs, such as social assistance (welfare) or other social supports. They are dependants who represent a large, complicated, and problematic expenditure for all levels of government.

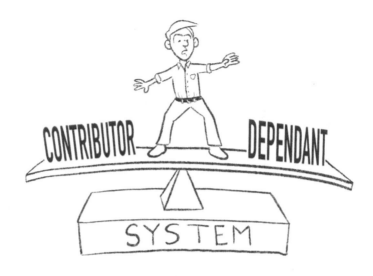

From an **individual perspective**, if someone is a government dependant, there is a greater likelihood that they (and their families) are living in poverty. Poverty brings challenges in basic stability, including such factors as precarious housing, food insecurity, physical and mental health issues, and low self-esteem. Making ends meet is an endless source of stress. Even if an unemployed person is not dependent on the system, unemployment often brings a sense of hopelessness to those who desperately want to contribute.

The price of opportunity lost is immeasurable. The impacts of long term unemployment are far-reaching, including poor retirement standards and impairment to the potential of the next generation. It is not just a *right now* problem.

From a **community perspective**, unemployment contributes to all manner of societal ills, including crime, violence, oppression, and marginalization. As family incomes are constricted, local business suffers. Communities begin to experience out-migration of residents seeking work, reducing both valuable potential and local spending. Communities become split between those *with* jobs (and therefore growth and opportunity) and those *without*, creating deep divides.

Lastly, from a **labour market perspective**, there are jobs without people and people without jobs.

What is going on?

There are many conflicting facts and opinions about what is going on. Do we have:

- Skill shortages?

- Labour shortages?

- Shortages of quality candidates?

- Shortages of quality jobs?

- A failing education system?

- Economic policy issues?

- A battle between "haves" and "have-nots"?

- Local or global issues?

- A question of societal ethics?

- Failure by the political far-left or the far-right?

- Structural oppression of visible minorities, women, Indigenous persons, and persons with disabilities?

Is it all these things, all at once?

We don't know.

What do we know?

What we do know with certainty is that decent employment builds sustainable communities and strong, safe, and healthy individuals and families. Equity and diversity create shared prosperity. **The employment problem is worth solving,** and governments across the globe are investing billions of dollars into local employment programs to do just that. Taxpayer-funded programs are intended to unlock the market for people who urgently want and need jobs, and to support employers to find and keep employees. Sounds good, right?

Can we talk?

Despite the billions invested, it isn't working, and we want to talk about it.

We believe that the employment systems and solutions created, herein referred to as the "employment services sector" (ESS), are largely **broken.** There is far too much money being spent and far too many players involved in what is essentially window dressing. It looks like we have a solution, but in practice, the most vulnerable people continue to be left behind. **The sector itself has become a significant barrier to employment for under-represented groups.** Ironically, it appears these tax-funded programs are most effective at creating sustainable employment for government and career development practitioners, because the evidence appears to show that they largely **do not** create sustainable employment for the populations of people they are intended to serve. *Ouch!*

Who the hell are we?

We, the authors—Sarah Delicate and Angela Hoyt—have collectively spent over sixty years gainfully employed in the employment services sector, primarily in Canada. We started as career development practitioners (CDP) and program managers, have both worked as organizational development specialists for government, and have both served as consultants in the employment services sector for the past two decades. Together, we bring a corporate memory that spans three decades of government-funded employment service programming and delivery. In that time, we have seen programs come and go, and come around again. We have seen the patterns repeat themselves with the same not-so-pretty results, with progressively more data to expose the illusion.

Despite our own Adverse Childhood Experiences (ACEs)[1], we are acutely aware of our privilege as white, Gen X, heterosexual, cisgender women. At our core is our common belief in and commitment to equity, inclusion, and belonging.

We are humbled and grateful to be acknowledged as experts in the employment and workforce development sector, and we have been fortunate to build lifetime careers in this area. Age and experience can bring wisdom, and it can also bring weariness and crankiness. We wish to share both our wisdom and our cranky.

---

1   PACEs Connection, 2021, www.acesconnectioninfo.com

You will not find much sugar coating in this book. We thank you in advance for being interested, open-minded, and tolerant, and for receiving the message in the spirit intended: continuous improvement.

WIDE-SWEEPING DISCLAIMER: In saying that things are broken, we are *not* saying that *everything* is broken. Some things *are* working, *some* of the time—we have seen it. But those things that are working are not systemic, not "scaled-up," not sustainable, and do not result in transformative and significant results to the populations of people about whom we are concerned. We welcome the opportunity to review any research that could demonstrate otherwise.

We still have optimism and hope. In fact, we are more optimistic than ever about the direction of workforce development. Never before have we seen such interest in labour market information and the future of work from so many players: government, employment service providers, education, industry, academia, evaluators, sector-specific associations, and business consultants. No doubt most of these players can see the reality of the situation and would like to be part of the solution.

We are not armed with a *silver bullet* that can address these challenges, but there are things we can and must do. We are going to talk about these while sharing a few shop secrets and stories. Here's how we are going to do it:

- We are going to look under the hood, share our observations, and invite you to reflect on your own context and practice.

- We are going to outline what we see as the root causes.

- We will present you with some potential solutions, which may be simple in theory but not easy in practice. And,

- We will invite you to consider your own way forward.

THE BIG WHY

Why are we doing this?

We've got nothing to lose and so much to gain for so many. As self-employed consultants and trainers, we can share our stories without the need for permissions. We answer to no one but ourselves. We've been there and we know, first-hand, the daily frustrations experienced as career development practitioners. Clients, too, are banging their heads—just on a different kind of wall.

The autumn of our careers looms, and we feel a need to document our corporate memory before it is lost. So, we are going out on a limb and cutting down a few trees, with hopes that this will be received in the spirit we intend. We hope you will find even one nugget of truth that will send you on a quest to look under your own hood and to implement small changes that will change lives, yours included.

CHAPTER 1:
Employment Services by Design

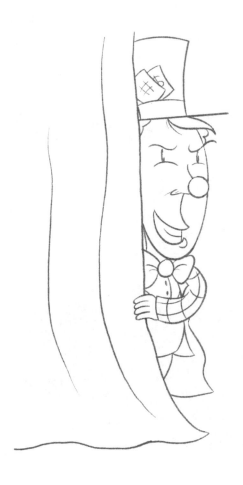

Employment Services by Design

*This chapter is a bit of a primer on the
employment services sector.*

W HEREVER YOU GO, anywhere in the world, community employment service programs look pretty much the same (and so do high school and post-secondary employment placement programs, by the way. They mostly include some degree of the same service interventions and pathways, and they mostly have the same desired outcome: sustainable employment for all job seekers, particularly those most distant from the labour market.

Although there may be different funders, program names, locations, and populations served, the *service pathway*—the route to sustainable employment—tends to be universal.

We designed the following diagram to illustrate a typical client/ job seeker service pathway, which includes various service functions (interventions and activities) starting from the left and, ideally, moving to the right.

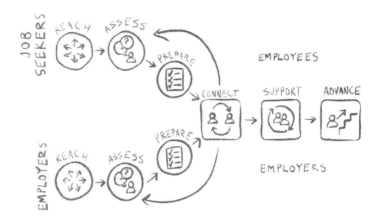

The Service Pathway

Most employment services include functions that focus on the supply (job seeker) side and functions that focus on the demand (employer) side of the employment service equation (from intake to outcome).

Supply-Side Functions: Interventions and activities that focus on **changing the job seeker** in some way before, during, or after employment.

Demand-Side Functions: Interventions and activities that focus on **influencing the employer's decision** to hire and retain the job seeker.

The usual employment service pathway is predominantly *supply-side functions* with *demand-side functions* nested within. The service pathway is not intended to represent the agency's organizational structure, or the *form*, of how the functions are delivered and who delivers them. Depending on the program, the government funder may even be prescriptive about the specific functions, form, or both.

These may be distinct job titles with distinct job functions, or one person may be required to do many of these functions under one job title.

For programs that have flexibility on *form* within their government contracts, organizations often ask us for formulas pertaining to staff–client ratios and employment counsellor (supply-side)–job developer (demand-side) ratios, and whether these staff roles should be blended together. Should we have ten employment counsellors and one job developer, or ten job developers with one employment counsellor? To their dismay, our answer is usually, "It depends."

What depends?

It depends on such things as the desired outcomes and design of the program, the population served, the labour market, and the competencies of the people doing the work. We do not advocate one organizational structure that fits all. What does your performance data currently tell you? We encourage *learning organizations* that adopt a continuous learning cycle: learning-adjusting-improving-learning (and throw in some "reflecting" in between).

As far as populations served, government-funded employment programs primarily focus on job seekers who are considered to be "employment-barriered"—those most *distant from the labour market,* such as persons with disabilities, racialized youth, newcomers to the country, etc.—as they may experience complex obstacles and needs. It must be stated that an employment-barriered population is not *homogeneous,* although it is often treated as such. There are sub-groups within each population, and there are sub-groups within sub-groups. For example, social assistance recipients (often known as "welfare recipients") range from someone who worked the same job for thirty years, was laid off, exhausted their employment insurance, and can't find a job, to the low-skilled, low literacy, multi-generational social assistance recipient who does not appear to want to work.

There may also be *intersectionality.* The *Oxford Dictionary* describes this as, "an interconnected nature of social categorizations such as race, class, and gender as they apply to a given individual or group . . . creating overlapping and interdependent systems of discrimination or disadvantage."[2] The client

2   "Intersectionality." *Oxford University Press, Lexico, 2021,* https://www. lexico.com/definition/intersectionality (accessed November 24, 2021).

could be a young, highly competent Indigenous female with two post-secondary degrees and a diagnosis of cerebral palsy. This is an example of why the ratios and allocation of resources within an organizational structure "depends."

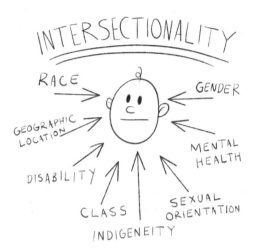

Job seekers have **unique** features that require **unique** interventions. While there are common features among job seekers on any counsellor's caseload, regardless of the population served, the population is not in the least homogeneous.

The following is a categorization of job seekers on a caseload, which some readers may find offensive or reductionist. However, it is not intended to classify people **as more- or less-than, or "othered," or to screen them in or out of service** (they've got enough of those screens to contend with). The sole purpose of this categorization is to highlight that job seekers have different strengths and needs and require different service interventions. Ultimately, this supports organizations to provide equitable and inclusive services.

 STARS: These job seekers have good qualifications and skills, are highly motivated to work, well educated, well connected, present well, and interview well. With little guidance, they will move swiftly through the employment service pathway and land a job on their own.

SUNS: These job seekers are motivated to work, skilled, and educated. They may have a few issues they need to work on, such as career exploration, job skills, their resume, and interview and other job-search skills. With some support, they will land a job on their own.

MOONS: This category is divided in two parts: the HALF-MOONS and FULL-MOONS.

- **HALF-MOONS:** These job seekers are very much like STARS and SUNS in that they are skilled, at least at a minimum level, and are motivated to work. What sets them apart is they have a visible "feature" that distinguishes them from other job seekers; for example, they are a racialized person or a person with a physical disability. They may have language skills challenges or have experienced a long employment gap. Again, they are *motivated to work*. For this job seeker, the barrier is often **the perception of the employer** that the job seeker is less than desirable. These job seekers often need a third party, such as a job developer, to open doors for them.

- **FULL-MOONS:** These job seekers face one or more barriers, such as low motivation to work, few apparent skills, or both. They may face such challenges as low literacy, poor communication skills, issues with personal hygiene, and/or have social problems that affect their ability to secure and retain a job.

FULL-MOONS are not likely to appeal to the average employer on the strength of their resume or interview skills. They may not appear motivated to attend job-search training and, like the HALF-MOONS, will need a third party to open doors for them. If they land a job, they may also require fairly intensive follow-up services.

 CLOUDS: These job seekers may be the most challenging clients for career practitioners. Chronically unemployed, they may not show up for interviews or jobs, or may quit the job after a short period of time. They may or may not have education and skills or visible employment barriers. Their defining feature is *they do not want to work, at all.* They may visit the employment service because they have been sent, under duress, by a parent, case worker, or probation officer. CLOUDS require a strategy that is typically not available in employment service programs: a cognitive-motivational model to develop problem-solving and social skills and to help them develop the intrinsic motivation to work.

It has been our experience that all employment service programs have clients that fit into these categories of differing needs. Understanding the needs composition of your caseload helps you design both your program and your staffing organizational design. For example, if a client caseload is predominantly comprised of the "almost ready to go" STARS and SUNS, an organizational structure focused on the supply-side (client interventions) will serve you well. If your caseload is predominantly MOONS (facing discrimination), a solely supply-focused organization will always fail because the issue is, in part, related to the demand-side, the employer.

Let's define "outcome-based," or "results-based," which we are using interchangeably. Outcome-based means that the government contract is not just measured by WHAT you do and HOW MUCH of it you do (e.g., opened 800 client files, conducted workshops), but WHAT CHANGES as a result of the work that you do. What is the impact of your activity on people and the community? Are more people who are typically left behind employed at liveable wages? Are more people literate? Are more people settled in Canada? **Outcome measures** describe what is to be changed, **outcome-based targets** lay out specifically how many measurable changes you are aiming for, and **outcome-based funding** means that stable funding requires you to achieve those outcomes.

LOGIC MODEL

Many outcome-based funding models use some version of a "logic model" to map out the logical progression required to reach the desired results. The Kellogg Foundation does a brilliant job of explaining logic models in their *Logic Model Development Guide* (W.K. Kellogg Foundation, 2004).[3]

---

3   W. K. Kellogg Foundation, *Logic Model Development Guide: Using Logic Models to Bring Together Planning, Evaluation, and Action*, (Battle Creek: W.K. Kellogg Foundation, 2004)

Performance is not measured by an exclusive focus on activity and intake, results, expenditures, or customer satisfaction, "success is measured by a combination of:

- Who is served (i.e., profile of suitability).

- What happens to them (i.e., outcome or impact of service).

- How well individuals and employers think they have been served (service coordination and customer satisfaction). And,

- The value for the investment (efficiencies)." [4]

As simple diagrams, logic models are just tidy program frameworks. Think of it this way:

We use our **resources/inputs** doing our day-to-day **activities**, which results in an **output** of products and services.

These outputs are tangible and would likely be outlined on a marketing brochure or website.

Over the short and long term, these outputs create intended CHANGES. These are the **outcomes**. Outcomes also progress. Short term changes first (knowledge, awareness, skills), which will lead to more intermediate change (behaviour change, change of status), which will then lead to broader, longer-term changes (societal changes).

---

4   Angela Hoyt, *Performance Management System for Service Delivery Site Managers* (Toronto: Ontario Ministry of Training Colleges and Universities, 2011), 29.

Outcomes

When a government-funding contract is outcome-based, there will be clear expectations and targets: how and when you spend your **inputs**, what and how many **activities** you do, what **outputs** you produce, and what **outcomes** you achieve. This is the business transaction: public tax dollars in exchange for meaningful change. If you cannot deliver on the agreement, you will not likely continue as a business partner. As a taxpayer, this makes a lot of sense.

If only it was as simple as the drawing of a logic model. Darn humans make this significantly more complicated.

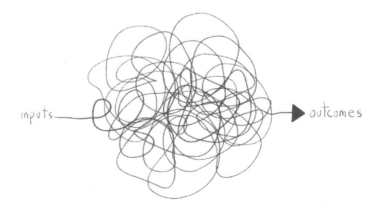

CHAPTER 2:

Drowning in the Survival Culture

CHAPTER 2:

Drowning in the Survival Culture

G OVERNMENTS ARE DRIVEN to tell a "Good News!" story within the confines of an election cycle. Irrespective of the political stripe, a key objective is always to build strong, safe, and healthy communities through increased employment. Elected officials have just four years to convince voters that they are doing a bang-up job.

In the name of that "Good News!" story, hard truths may be swept under the carpet unless an external auditor hauls them out into the light. The threat of Open Data, Open Information, and Open Government are terrifying, as they uncover and make accessible the actual performance stories of some government programs. Data paid for by the people belongs to the people. In some countries, unspent annual program dollars drive fear into the hearts of program managers and government departments alike ("Bad News!"). The culture of spreading "Good News!" stories and maintaining a structure where all dollars must be spent within the contract period (*spend it or you lose it*) can have a downside. The well-intended spirit of policy and program design can, in some cases, be severely compromised.

To keep their annual funding, organizations are driven to tell the story their funders need to hear. The performance of these organizations is measured, tracked, and scored to death, such that the reporting may in and of itself become an impediment to quality service. Easily measured performance targets (e.g., the absence or presence of a job) are imposed within formidable performance frameworks—yet program values, principles, quality, and long term outcomes are rarely measured.

Under the guise of greater demands for accountability and transparency, the new norm for some employment programs can be ever-increasing caseloads, onerous and controlling paperwork, restrictive operating dollars, and expanding rules, regulations, and restrictions.

"**Accountabalism**" (being eaten alive by attempted precision) assumes perfection in program policy, processes, and procedures while at the same time removing and restricting human judgment.[5] If the organization does not hit the prescribed performance and financial targets, they will be sacrificed to the audit gods (with the exception of election years, when governments would be loath to close an employment program). This breeds a *fear-based survival culture.*

As consultants to the field, we provide support to employment organizations that are struggling to hit their government-imposed targets and thereby struggling to keep their funding. In our respective and joint journeys down this long and winding road, we have gathered stories that make our heads spin. We have met wonderful people, all over Canada, in all positions, who are under similar pressures but have different responses.

We have seen situations that, if unveiled, would infuriate funders and make agency directors shake in their boots. Such

---

5   David Weinberger, "The Folly of Accountabalism," *Harvard Business Review*, February, 2007.

practices can be said to fall on a spectrum between somewhat unethical to outright fraud.

We regularly uncover practices agencies use (consciously or not) to survive another day and year, to make it appear that they are fulfilling their contractual obligations. Upon closer inspection (and it doesn't have to be that close), performance is often superficial. These *survival* practices are found in **fear-based work cultures**. "In a fear-based culture, the desire to look good—or not to look bad—can take precedence over the business objectives at hand . . . Fear creates interference which prevents people and organizations from reaching their full potential."[6]

In employment service agencies, a *survival culture* breeds one behaviour more than any other: a dysfunctional, vicious cycle of ***hitting the targets but missing the point.*** This is done on the backs of the most vulnerable job seekers, who are almost always the intended benefactors of these government-funded programs.

Ultimately, achieving the contracted results for clients facing the most complex employment barriers is often seen as an impossibility. Some agencies find creative ways to "hit" the targets, working with easy-to-serve job seekers through a practice known as "creaming." These easy-to-serve job seekers come to the table with strong skills and experience. Employers are often looking for just these people. Even without the help of the

---

6   Timothy Gallwey, The Inner Game of Work: Focus, Learning, Pleasure, and Mobility in the Workplace (New York: Random House, 2001), 30.

employment service centre, these **STARS** and **SUNS** would have eventually found jobs on their own. Some find jobs as quickly as it takes to fill out the paperwork to report on the success. They are a quick and easy and well-executed employment outcome statistic. Yay!

This is not the case with "hard-to-serve" job seekers. In addition to the *personal* barriers they may face, such as low income or disability, these "hard-to-serve" job seekers come to the table lacking skills and experience, or, even worse, they face *systemic* barriers, not only from employers, but from  the very employment service whose sole purpose is to help them. "Oh, we are not a placement agency! Don't expect a job on a silver platter. We are here to TEACH you how to find a job so next time you are looking for one, you won't need our help." (Yes, common story. Yes, infuriating.)

What's that all about?

Government-funded employment agencies will likely always be impacted by an election cycle, measured ad nauseam, and forced to achieve mandated outcomes and spend all allocated funding or face the loss of future program funding. Yes, governments need "Good News!" stories, and your agency needs to survive, but it needs to survive without forgetting why it exists. This requires a shift out of a fear-based survival culture into a *culture of right action.*

We have coined the term "Bullsh*t Practices", which are *some* of the most common survival practices we often see on the ground (and often evidenced in data, if you know where and what to look for). Not all of these practices are applicable to all program designs, but if there are workarounds, a struggling organization may conclude it has no choice but to use them, especially if they know (or perceive) other service providers are already using them.

We'd like to introduce you to "The Bull" who headlines our next chapter.

CHAPTER 3:

*Bullsh*t Survival Practices*

CHAPTER 3:

*Bullsh*t Survival Practices*

W HILE THE NAMES of the practices may be tongue-in-cheek, the content is non-fiction and may be surprising or even shocking to some. Sometimes these practices are in play because the agency hasn't had time to step back and reflect on how it is achieving its targets; sometimes it's because individual staff members feel pressure to report results creatively to maintain their own employment.

Regardless of the reason, it is **not our intention** to teach unethical practices. These practices are outlined in case a kernel of truth can be extracted that will help put agency practices under a microscope, help take a closer look at what may be happening, and then help find another, more ethical way of operating.

Let's be super-duper clear, this is **not a playbook** to be added to already unethical practices. We believe awareness can be curative—so a huge gold star if we bump you from **unconscious incompetence** to **conscious incompetence** (*Yay you!*). It is our hope that this will raise awareness of practices you may not even be aware are happening in your organization. (Hint: They are more prevalent as the fiscal year draws to a close.)

So, without further ado, here are the "Bullsh*t Survival Practices." They are sorted by these headings: **Intake, Non-Intake, Exit, Post-Exit Follow-Up**, and **Spend the Money**. Sadly, these headings are not mutually exclusive.

BULLSH*T CLIENT INTAKE

Intake: This is the number of clients formally enrolled in a program, usually with a needs assessment and a service plan.

On the ground, this process starts with a program registration form and a discussion about the service and ends with the data on the form being entered into the government information system. It is the *let's work together* handshake. Unless told otherwise, the client probably thinks, "I'm in. You've got my back."

1. **Doughnuts and Coffee Intake:** One of the authors ran a job club program in the 90s, which was federally funded based on the number of "bums in seats." In a world before outcome targets, the staff had only

to set up the chairs in a horseshoe formation and lay the doughnuts beside the registration sheet to be able to report that a group had been run. It didn't matter that half of the class generally would not benefit from the class (working under the table, severe addictions, etc.), as long as bums were in seats for the roll call.

Luring people into an agency with light snacks or a free newspaper has been successful for decades.

2. **Tombstone Intake:** Collect just enough information (name, date of birth, etc.) to open a file and make the person a program statistic in the system but provide no actual service.

3. **Bait and Capture Intake:** Advertise a "job" or "job fair" online. Dozens to hundreds of people apply and fill out the agency intake form (a prerequisite for attendance), thus all becoming counted as "job seekers" in the program!

4. **Leapfrog Intake:** Multi-service agencies funded by multiple sources (government, grants, associations, etc.) map out intakes across different programs, such that every client is a potential source of multiple intake "ticks" across programs.

   For example, do you want to attend the new retail services program funded by the city? Your first stop is a nationally funded employment counselling program; second stop, a locally funded job club; third stop, the textile association's new sewing program; and fourth stop, the retail services program (finally!). You go in for one program and the agency receives credit for four intakes and outcomes. Yay!

5. **Washroom Intake:** "But I just came to use the washroom!" *Sign here please.* Everyone walking in the building, from the plumber to the government funding representative, has to sign in, not for

security reasons, but for performance "points." Even we, as consultants, have been counted in the organizations we have visited.

6. **Strategic Pulse Intake:** Intake all job seekers with a pulse, as long as the "easiest to serve" clients (the 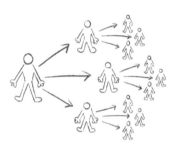 SUNS and STARS) will hit the employed outcome targets and the "difficult" clients (the MOONS and CLOUDS) fall within your "negative outcome allowance." This is just about math.

7. **Exponential Intake:** The intake numbers include the same person accessing the service over and over, only the client doesn't know it. Open and close and open the files again within the timeframes that allow  for the maximum intake count (for example, three months), without the job seeker's knowledge or consent.

One of the authors worked with one agency where forty percent of their intake numbers were achieved with this clever little trick.

8. **Lucrative Loiterers:** These are the "job seekers" who have been visiting the resource centre for years. The centre provides a social environment that is warm in winter, cool in summer, and has doughnuts and free access to computers. *"I have no real intention of securing employment and you have no real intention of helping me, but I will sign your paperwork and your agency will get paid."* While it is heart-warming for your

agency to provide shelter for these people in need (we agree this is good community service, but probably not your agency's mandate), this type of dishonest intake reporting is definitely "gaming."

9. **Turnstile Intake:** Some programs allow for one client to be counted multiple times a day—and counted they are. Client looks out the window, tick! Goes for a coffee, tick! Goes to the washroom, tick!

10. **Frequent Flyer Intake:** These are job seekers that live a life of seasonal employment, sometimes due to the realities of the local labour market; other times, it's a lifestyle choice. Whatever the reason, they get laid off at the end of every season. To sustain their employment insurance, they need to demonstrate they are looking for work, and that's where the employment agency comes in. These are easy intake pickings every year: same people, same subsidy, same precarious employment, no long term, sustainable employment plan.

11. **Program Parking Intake:** While some programs only count clients who have exited the service, others count clients when the file is open. And if that file runs over fiscal years, these same clients are counted year after year.

In this environment, the job seeker is parked in training or in counselling for years and never given the opportunity to go to work. Unfortunately, persons with disabilities are commonly served in this way. Case in point— ask an unemployed person using a wheelchair about their multiple post-secondary degrees and how often, and how well, they have been served by employment service organizations.

12. **Drop and Dash or Place and Pray Intake:** After you introduce the job seeker to the employer, the employer hires them because they believed you when you said the job seeker is the "perfect" candidate . . . but then you never contact the employer again. What was your problem is now the employer's problem. If the client loses their job and comes back for service—Score!—another intake number.

BULLSH*T NON-INTAKE (CREAMING)

Non-Intake: Similar to intake, the client fills out the registration form (or they are not invited to complete it at all, even if they are eligible and suitable for the program), but that form is not actually entered into the government information system. Because they are not told otherwise, the job seeker assumes they are a client of the service. This person is typically unaware that they are not formally in the program, or they are simply redirected elsewhere.

1. **Specialized Rejection Non-Intake:** Even though the agency is promoted as a "one stop" service provider, job seekers with disabilities, newcomers, and Indigenous persons are directed to the very small agency in town that "specializes" in serving those populations. Yes, some programs do specialize in some populations, but this happens even in programs that are intended to serve all job seekers. These clients are redirected, not necessarily to serve their best interest, but to preserve

the agency's impressive record of successful employed-outcome stats.

2. **Policy Rejection Non-Intake:** Intake staff are trained to filter out job seekers that will be difficult to employ. Job seekers are told that they are not eligible for service due to government regulations (that the government is  not aware of, of course). *Sorry, we would* REALLY *like to serve you, but you need to have been out of work for three months. Or, out of school. Or, in school. Or, have come in the week before. Or, be a youth. Or, an older worker. Or, be a unicorn.*

BULLSH*T EMPLOYMENT OUTCOMES

Employment outcomes are just that: the person who came in looking for work, or looking for less precarious work, is now working. Some programs also have "quality" measures, such as wages, work hours, benefits, etc. **Educational outcomes are also measures of success in many government-funded employment programs; however, we are focusing exclusively on the employment outcomes.** Employment outcomes usually trigger an **exit.**

Exit: This is like when a patient's wristband is removed during a hospital discharge and the person is no longer a patient. For the majority of clients, the "band" is removed  because they have achieved the outcome of landing a job: they no longer "belong" to the service. Exit triggers post-exit follow-up.

Post-Exit Follow-Up: The agency follows up with the client at a predetermined time (usually within the first year) to check if they are still employed, and if not, they may invite the client back to the service—Bonus intake!—or refer them to another service.

It's often hard to get in touch with a client after they leave a service. Whether they have moved, changed their phone number, or just ghosted you, you need to document an outcome, which can lead to some pretty creative conclusions.

Here are some examples of the classic Bullsh*t Employment Outcomes:

1. **The Footwear Job:** I saw them in town with work boots on, and the boots were dirty. They must be working! Tick.

2. **The Missed Phone Call Job:** I called them twice between 8:30 a.m. and 4:30 p.m., and they did not answer. Duh! Working! Tick.

3. **The Family Services Job:** I called, and they were babysitting for their sister. Score! Working! Tick.

4. **The Facebook Job:** I saw a picture of them on Facebook, and they clearly looked like they were working. Tick.

5. **The Sneeze Job:** The job seeker accepted a job and gets counted even if they never showed up to the job or only sneezed on it and left. Tick.

Another example, based on the other five times the client received services from the agency (*Yay, five intakes*): It is known that this client can get a job but not keep a job—or they keep it for a week before they quit or get fired, again. *Quick, close their file before they lose this one.* Tick.

Or, is this an employer with extremely high turnover? (Talkin' to you, call centres and retail and restaurant chains.) *Quick, close the file!* Tick.

Or, did your client land a short, seasonal job? Close file to "employed" before the strawberries are all picked. Tick.

6. **The Strategic Seasonal Job:** If the employed outcome is measured at a three-month follow-up, time this strategically: exit the client to "unemployed" in March, and then close to "employed" in June, when they are, once again, precariously employed picking strawberries and living below the poverty line. Tick.

The bonus hustle of the Bullsh*t **Frequent Flyer Intake** is to open the client's file every season, provide little service, but collect the outcome stat. Just give the employer a subsidy when the client goes back to the same seasonal job they've had for 10 years running. Tick.

7. **The Miracle Jobs:** The agency has very high employment outcomes for clients with severe and multiple employment barriers, and they achieved it in a *fraction* of the time it takes compared to other employment agencies. *It's a miracle!* Tick.

Tip: This is potentially an early-warning sign of fraud.

It's just so easy to tick the boxes in the suitability indicators to make someone *look* really "barriered" on paper when maybe they aren't. Or maybe they *are* that "barriered" and the jobs are not real. For example, one concerned agency director contracted one of the authors to do a forensic data audit on an employment counsellor, as their stats appeared too good to be true—and they were. The employment outcomes in the files were all fabricated. The counsellor was escorted out the door, and the funder was notified of the fraud. *Ouch!*

8. **The Hack Job:** The agency convinces the employer to split one job amongst five clients with disabilities (which is a major problem when clients are capable of working full time). Each client gets one day of the job per week, the agency gets five times the stats, and the employer gets five times the money. Tick, tick, tick, tick, tick, and cha-ching!

9. **The Snow Job:** This one is really cool because the agency has an accomplice: the employer. When the agency "secures" a job for their client, they then sign up the employer's existing staff as a new client and give the employer a wage subsidy for both of them. Bonus intake and two employment outcomes. Tick. Tick.

Yes, this actually happens. Yes, it's fraud.

10. **Process, Park, and Pray Job:** You take clients through the intake interview, get them to fill out the registration form (wonder who will ever hire them), enter the client data into the information system, provide no service, light a candle, and pray they find their own way. Triple points if they do find a job and get personal and employer incentives. Close the file to "employed," pat yourself on the back, and do a happy dance.

11. **Spaghetti Job:** The employer thinks you are "pre-screening" job candidates, but really you are sending them the resumes of anyone and everyone. Like throwing spaghetti on the wall, you pray that one sticks.

12. **The Sleight-of-Hand Job:** The agency meets the funder's employment outcome targets by maintaining two different sets of filing cabinets: one invisible filing cabinet for the job seekers  that they do not expect to be successful (MOONS and CLOUDS), and the other visible filing cabinet for those the agency predicts will lead to a quick employment outcome (STARS and SUNS). The agency only "opens" the job seekers in the government information system who they predict will be successful, while parking others in the invisible filing cabinet. Magic! The funders see nothing but success!

    If clients in the invisible filing cabinet actually do land jobs on their own (yay!), they are moved over to the visible cabinet . . . Abracadabra!

    Aside from being morally reprehensible, the two filing cabinets also severely hamper the professional's ability to do their jobs. And they are often "serving" (read "processing") two or more times the number of clients than the agency is funded to serve. For example, if the agency is funded to serve a caseload of 120 clients, some staff have actual caseloads of 250 clients: 120 clients in the visible files, 130 clients in the invisible files. Their actual capacity to help people has been cut in half. It's a vicious cycle, as they can't give the people that are most often left behind, those in the invisible filing cabinet, the attention they need. In their neglect, everyone fails: the client, the staff person, the agency, the potential employer, and the community. But it's a "Good News!" story.

BULLSH*T SPEND THE MONEY

Spend the money: Money is received from the funder to deliver the program as contracted. "Operational" funds cover the "bricks and mortar" to deliver the program. In some programs, operational funds are *pay for performance*, similar to a base salary job with commission incentives.

In some programs, *flow-through* funds are assigned to employers to offset wages/training costs and/or for client supports; for example, reimbursement for transportation, day care, safety boots, etc. If the *flow-through* money is not spent by the end of the fiscal year, the agency risks losing it the following year. This fuels the perennial *use it or lose it* strategy.

Classic Bullsh*t Spend the Money practices include:

1. **Fill the Order:** This is a common strategy for agencies looking to spend the money by filling jobs they don't have clients readily available for. Perhaps their existing caseload  of job seekers is largely seeking administration jobs, but the agency keeps getting requests from employers for trades or engineering jobs. When employers have these types of jobs available, the agency, wanting to boost their employed outcomes and spend their money, may advertise them online—and dozens to hundreds of

people apply. This is problematic, and a little unethical in our opinion, as the employment service is contracted to land jobs for the people on their caseloads (especially the MOONS), not people for jobs (the STARS, for whom the service is rarely intended).

"But wait," you may say, "employers are our customers too!" or, "But those people need to find work too!" Yes, this is true, but ask yourself, are these your *primary customers?* Primary customers are those for whom your program is designed—the intended benefactors who need your help the most. "Oh right," you may say, "never mind." A government-funded employment agency is not like a private-sector recruiter, looking to fill any job with any applicant. There are whole industries of job board sites and recruiters for that.

2. **Corporate Welfare:** Employers are given wage incentives to hire people they would have hired anyway. Sometimes, they even come to you and say, "Hey, I'm going to hire this very shiny person. How much can you give me?"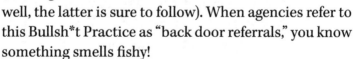

   Note, the employment service programs highlighted in this book are focused on *workforce development*, not *economic development* (although if the former is done well, the latter is sure to follow). When agencies refer to this Bullsh*t Practice as "back door referrals," you know something smells fishy!

3. **Best Friend Employer/Private Membership Placements:** The agency is hitting all their placement/ employment targets, and they are spending all their money. However, if you look beneath the surface, they

seem to partner with the same one to five employers, over and over. In some cases, these same employers are also getting money from the other service providers in town. If you take a closer look, you will see these employers typically offer low-skilled, low-pay, precarious jobs.

If the sum total of the "free" government money received by these employers (and their incredible staff turnover) ever hit the cover of a major newspaper, it would be scandalous.

4. **Pay Equity for Employers:** Every employer gets the maximum amount of money, whether the client needs it or not. *Oh, the client only needs three hours of training? It's your lucky day, 16 weeks of wage subsidy for you!*

5. **Buy One, Get Many Free:** When the employer hires one of the agency's clients, the agency will register and give the employer a subsidy for all their EXISTING staff, in some cases falsifying and back-dating documents. See "Snow Job" under Bullsh*t Outcomes.

6. **The Serial Subsidy Employer:** This is the employer who hires a client with the maximum wage subsidy. Everything is going swimmingly, the employer frequently reports all is going well, and everyone is happy. Then, wonder of wonders, just before the subsidy ends, the client is fired for being a disaster. Then the employer asks: "Do you have another?" "And, another?" "How about another?"

(Seriously, WHY do you keep working with these employers?)

7. **STAR or SUN Self-Placer:** The SUNS and STARS attach a letter to their resume provided by the agency, to inform the employers that if they hire them, "free" money will be given to them. Therefore, the money intended to offset training costs for MOONS has been doled out for people (STARS and SUNS) who would have been hired anyway and didn't need it in the first place.

Historically, training and wage subsidies have been used as a strategy to convince employers to hire job seekers with employment barriers when the real intent was to close gaps in training and experience for the MOONS and CLOUDS. This strategy has prompted employers AND employment service providers to view these job seekers as deficient—so *broken* that employers had to be paid to hire them. In recent years, because employers have come to expect government grants and because agencies are penalized for not spending the money, the original intent of the subsidy has been lost. Now, staff get frustrated that employers don't want the money, but they have to convince them to take it anyway(!). Recently, a staff person told one of the authors, in a group training session, that her manager instructed her to tell employers that the agency had "oodles of money" that her agency had to "get rid of," to which the manager replied defensively, "I never told you to say that!" with the staff person looking at her in disbelief. This was not the first time we have heard a similar refrain.

8. **Intervention Cost Rigging:** Everyone gets the same interventions regardless of their needs, billed at the highest rate (when interventions are separately priced and paid for by governments). Hit the numbers, spend money, and get money, on the backs of the most vulnerable because there is often no time or money left for them.
But . . . but, we have to get our numbers and spend the money or we will be out of business! (Um, if you focus on what job seekers truly need, the results will follow.)

Sometimes, and none too often, we see agencies using only one or two of these **Bullsh*t Survival Practices (BSSPs)** because they are struggling to achieve results in just one performance measurement target, such as Intake. Most often, we see several **BSSPs** in play and, when combined, the target is hit in more than one performance measure—we call these **Super Bullsh*t Survival Practices (SBSSPs).** Like kale is considered a super-food, with all its wonderful attributes—low cal, high protein, fibre, multiple vitamins, folate, and more—a **SBSSP** breathes life into all three performance measurement categories: Intake, Outcome, and Spend the Money. Those **Super Bullsh*t Practices** pack a punch! *Ta-da!*

SUMMARY

All of these Bullsh*t Survival Practices, and others, play out year over year over year, across programs, across funders, and across jurisdictions. So, if some of these Bullsh*t Survival Practices are in play in your community and workplace, know that you are not alone. Sadly, this has been going on for decades. (And, since you forked over the money to pay for this book and you have read this far, you are probably infuriated by them too and ready to forge a new, more meaningful and impactful path.)

Sadly, the Bullsh*t Practices are global. Case in point, the Organisation for Economic Co-operation and Development's

(OECD) 2005 *Employment Outlook Report* (Yep! Pushing 20 years ago! AND STILL IN PRACTICE) references the broad employment service sector's use of **gaming, parking,** and **creaming**:

". . . employment service providers must be given broad-ranging responsibility for clearly defined groups of clients, and institutional arrangements must prevent 'gaming' (artificial manipulation of outcome measures) and 'creaming' (provider failure to enroll disadvantaged clients)."[7]

This report speaks to the observed practices in several OECD countries and uses jargon that is understood by almost everyone in the employment services sector. It is pretty sad that 1) these terms are widely used and familiar; and 2) that they are happening at all (still!). Despite the billions of dollars that are

---

7   Organisation for Economic Co-operation and Development,
     Employment Outlook Report 2005 (Paris: OECD Publishing, 2005), 209.

invested in workforce development, the "pros" just can't get it together. *Sheesh!*

A quick Google search of **gaming, parking,** and **creaming** revealed results such as:

- "'Parking' and 'Creaming' are endemic concerns within… welfare-to-work (WTW) systems internationally."[8]

- "The Work Programme's only success is at 'creaming and parking': The payment-by-results model means 'job-ready' job seekers are being helped more than those in need, costing more long term."[9] *Ouch!*

Clearly, there is a general consensus that **gaming, parking,** and **creaming** are the *dark side* of poor policy, rigid program design, and punitive performance measurement.

We know that most people are inherently good and that they wish to be successful in their jobs—and they depend on government funding, believe their hands are tied (and they often are), and therefore feel pressured to (literally) play the game. When facing the threat of failure, it is a pretty human response to find ways to succeed, even if it means *hitting the targets but missing the point.*
People convince themselves that they just won't get caught. When they realize they are fully engaged in these practices, they often become extremely demoralized, as it is

8   Eleanor Carter, Adam Whitworth, "Creaming and Parking in Quasi-Marketised Welfare-to-Work Schemes: Designed Out Of or Designed In to the UK Work Programme?" The Journal of Social Policy 44, no. 2 (April 2015): 277, https://doi.org/10.1017/S0047279414000841.

9   Richard Johnson, "The Work Programme's only success is at 'creaming and parking'," The Guardian, February 20, 2013, https://www.theguardian.com/commentisfree/2013/feb/20/work-programme-success-creaming-parking.

usually a sense of purpose that attracted them to the field in the first place. (It certainly wasn't the salary!) And the more demoralized and disengaged they become, the harder it is to pull themselves out of the vicious cycle.

The **Bullsh*t Survival Practices** are often evident in the data, if funders and service providers know where to look, and care to look. We, the authors, know where to look because we have trained many agencies and governments to find the telltale data patterns (and because one of the authors eats data for breakfast, lunch, and supper).

The response we often hear when we expose these practices is some version of: "Oh dang, busted! But it is just to get us through this year . . . We had two staff go off on sick leave/

there was a bus strike/we had to close for a week because of bed bugs . . . but next year, we will get back on track. Next year, for sure . . . just as soon as we get out from under this very threatening cloud of defunding."

In the meantime, despite the billions spent by taxpayers, those who need employment services the most continue to be left behind. *Fug.*

CONFESSION SECTION

It's fess up time! Now that you know what you know, it's time to reflect on your own **Bullsh*t Survival Practices,** or practices you have ignored. You may want to write in pencil if you could only afford one book for the office. If you bought the book yourself, you deserve a raise!

I recognize these Bullsh*t practices exist:

- ✓ Yes

- ✓ No

- ✓ I have no idea and/or I don't want to know

Here are some other practices that are prevalent in the sector that are not listed here:

_____

_____

_____

_____

If you are feeling consciously incompetent (you now know what you didn't know)—Congratulations! You get a gold star. Awareness can be curative, and just by being aware, you may already be on your way to fixing things. *Yay you!*

If you are in the "Ya, but . . ." place right now (yes, there is a lot out of your control, you can't fix a system that doesn't want to be fixed), consider: If this is your reality, what are you going to do about it?

A space for deep thoughts:

CHAPTER 4:

The Root Causes of Smoke and Mirrors

CHAPTER 4:

The Root Causes of Smoke and Mirrors

While there are many root causes of the Illusion, we believe the following are the hot ones!

CAUSE #1: GOVERNMENT SOUND BITES TRUMP SERVICE EXCELLENCE

It appears to be the expectation that if government-elected officials publicly announce a "shiny new" employment program on a Monday, service providers will have it up and running by Tuesday, and they will provide a positive performance report by Friday. Programs are not often supported with well-developed policy or meaningful training, as it is simply expected that programs already have the capacity. Removed from the government policy branches, the public servants tasked with rolling out the shiny new program may be as ill-informed about the program design, or intent, as the service providers funded to deliver them.

GOOD NEWS! Today, our government is publicly announcing a new employment program for the most popular (yet not evidence-based) issue of the day! We have carefully chosen the existing network of employment service providers that did not have to compete for this contract because who has time for that level of rigour? Because we did not consult with them in advance, they do not currently know anything about this program, but we are confident that they will be up and running by next Tuesday, and we will have our first wildly successful and grossly manipulated PDF-formatted performance scorecard out to you, our public, by the following Thursday. *Why are we so confident?* Because these service providers rely on us for their very existence, and we know that they will be happy to help us launch this very timely and critical election announceable. Six months from now, when data tells us that we got the policy all wrong, we will simply change the program rules through a memo, and these very nimble service providers will happily and instantly tell their job seekers and employers that they no longer qualify for funding, programming, or both. *Oh wait . . . now you do. Now you don't . . . do . . . don't . . .* This program uncertainty builds great resiliency into our labour market and our most vulnerable populations!

Over the last decade, the protective moat separating government public servants and the elected politician seems to have dried up. There was a time when social programs were designed and developed without political interference, based on genuine public need, supported by sound research. All too often, we now find programming-by-election-promise: programs announced with much fanfare, aligned with election cycles. Untested program policy is launched, without the benefit of pilots or even a preliminary discussion with the service providers destined to deliver them. Promising practices supported by research are ignored, **even if that funder paid for the research.**

In the name of efficiency, public programs may be launched with such speed that very little time and money are put into such things as effective roll-out strategies, consultation, change management, capacity building, and so on. Ultimately, this has the potential to be disastrously inefficient, as program success is elusive. Lacking internal training and support, government staff may be presented as the "go-to" experts in a program they don't understand, which could result in inconsistent policy application across geographical regions and indefensible monitoring practices. Ooops.

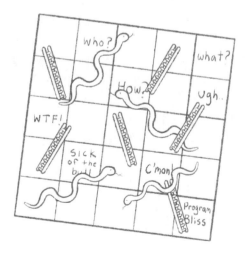

Training for service providers, *when provided,* is limited and often restates readily available written policy or program guidelines. Service providers are left with many questions, and clear answers are difficult to get, with endless redirection from the funder to re-read the program guidelines that left service providers wanting in the first place. Training rarely includes explanations such as WHO the program is for, WHY it is needed, WHAT values will guide the program roll out, HOW monitoring and evaluation will assess progress against the purpose, and what research supports the program design. Missing the who, why, what, and how results in a whole lot of "What the Fug?" These omissions allow a whole lot of **Hitting the Targets but Missing the Point (HTTBMTP)** causing **Super Bullsh*t Survival Practices (SPSSP)** to flourish because the "point" is nebulous.

Government staff turnover is rampant, sometimes resulting in a loss of corporate knowledge and memory. The government-

espoused principles and theories of evidence-based "continuous improvement" have in some cases been replaced by intense political pressure to demonstrate quick wins to the taxpayers, **now.** The mantra of "spend the money, fill the seats, get the numbers, and submit your reports" fuels a pervasive **fear-based culture of survival.** Service providers are frequently asked for, and have no choice but to deliver on, the funder's urgent requests for statistical information. Yet, this urgency may not always be reciprocated when service providers have pressing questions to support them to deliver the program. There is a lot of "hurry up and wait" going on.

Rushing out a new program without the benefit of consultation and support AND expecting *real* results with the *targeted* job seekers in the timelines required **is SIMPLY**

impossible and inadvisable, in our humble opinion. In quick order, a network of employment service providers may find themselves in the unenviable, if not to mention unethical, position of being reduced to **gaming, parking,** and **creaming** while the funder ignores and sometimes even encourages it. ("Um, maybe just count that employed outcome twice, so you and the other service provider both get the credit.")

Capacity is further diminished if staff on both the government and service delivery sides become so demoralized and discon-nected from their respective purposes that they jump ship, leaving substantial capacity gaps that further compound the issue. For those who choose to stay, employee engagement can suffer, and there is a risk that they become disengaged completely: *I quit! But I forgot to tell you, and I am still coming in, and you are still paying me* . . . Attracting new, qualified talent for this environment can be difficult.

As the shiny new employment program flounders, matures, and falls from the media's eye, or when it catches the attention of a merciless auditor or evaluator, efforts may then be made to pull the program out of this unethical tailspin. Sometimes, resuscitation interventions work, and the program begins to stabilize and improve as governments invest in consultation, capacity building, and evidence-based policy reviews. Other times, there is a "slash and burn" of service providers and service provider funding for those unable to demon-strate the required outcomes, or a complete cancellation of the program (often by a new government, who is not shy about pinning the failure on the last government). Not only were the employment problems NOT solved, millions upon millions of dollars were wasted due to a failed program launch.

CAUSE #2: ACCOUNTABILITY GONE WRONG

Increased Accountability Not Matched with Increased Flexibility

The Auditor General of Canada put out a paper in 2002 called *Modernizing Accountability in the Public Sector*.[10] And while 2002 may not be considered modern times (unless you are still rocking out to boy band NSYNC), the paper still holds true today because it is both useful and simple.

The paper defines accountability as "a relationship based on obligations to demonstrate, review and take responsibility for performance, both the results achieved in light of agreed expectations and the means used."[11] That sounds about right for the typical government transfer agreements and contracts with third-party employment services organizations.

It then goes on to say:

"Increased flexibility is often provided in exchange for greater accountability. More discretion in the use of authority and reasonable flexibility to make informed decisions about:

- The resources and inputs used

---

10   Auditor General of Canada, *2002 Report of the Auditor General of Canada to the House of Commons, Chapter 9: Modernizing Accountability in the Public Sector—December* (Ottawa: Minister of Public Works and Government Services, 2002).

11   Ibid, 1.

- The outputs to produce, and

- The way they are produced

A move to greater discretion, flexibility, and innovation is not supported by accountability that focuses solely on complying with too many and unneeded rules and procedures."[12]

Understanding this is critical, as it gives a tremendous amount of insight into what sometimes goes very wrong in the employment sector today. In exchange for greater accountability and more stringent and specific outcomes, the government must, in our opinion, give employment service organizations the agility and freedom to figure out how they are going to achieve outcomes, **as long as practices are legal and ethical.**

Question for the reader: In your current role, be it in government, non-profit, management, or front line, have you been given the professional autonomy to figure out HOW you are going to achieve your outcomes, or are you told what to do so there is no room for flexibility? See banana bread recipe below.

THE BANANA BREAD RECIPE (FOR DISASTER)

Imagine we, the authors, have contracted you to make banana bread. Within our contract, we have not only provided you with the precise, step-by-step recipe (Operational Guidelines with pictures), but we have also told you exactly what kitchen tools to utilize (to be verified by audit), what brand of ingredients to purchase (with a minimum of three quotes as per the financial directive),

---

12 Auditor General of Canada, *2002 Report of the Auditor General of Canada, Chapter 9: Modernizing Accountability—December,* (Ottawa: Minister of Public Works and Government Services, 2002), 5.

the exact temperature your eggs and butter must be (to be tracked in our data system), and exactly how and how long you are to mix the ingredients (ten folds, ten stirs). Eighty-five percent of all persons eating your banana bread must rate their satisfaction as a four or higher on a five-point scale. If you do not achieve this rating, you will lose your contract.

You follow the instructions EXACTLY. All audits indicate that you did exactly as you were told. If your banana bread is not well received (sixty percent rating, or an average rating of three out of five), **who is to blame? Can you be held accountable?**

While this may be an outlandish example, it is this same behaviour that we often see from government funders in employment service programming. They want to hold service providers to very precise and measurable outcomes (as they should!), but then they shackle them with unnecessary rules and processes and bury them with administrative requirements. The ability to be responsive, flexible, and nimble to changing populations, local labour markets, and evolving economic conditions is severely restricted.

What might this look like on the ground?

The government funder hinges the service provider's sustained contract on the EXACT outcomes that are to be achieved within a contract year.

For example:

Annual Performance Measurement Framework (to be formally assessed quarterly):

1. Open 480 "marginalized" client files (with a complex rating system to prove you are working with only marginalized clients, however defined)

2. Deliver 24 workshops to 480 job seekers

3. <u>Close</u> 800 client files within 12 months

4. Place 60% of clients into subsidized job placements

5. Spend 100% of your wage subsidy dollars within the fiscal year

6. Achieve a 70% employment outcome, whereby the client holds that job for at least 3 months

7. Achieve an 85% satisfaction rating from employers and clients

If these outcomes are not achieved, the contract may not be extended.

The funder is well within their rights to clearly define the expectations and the consequences of not achieving their prescribed outcomes. Through "negotiations" (they are often directions, not negotiations), the employment service provider can decide if they agree to the terms for the funding provided. Are you in or are you out? Do you know what you have signed up for?

Where the accountability relationship can go wrong is that many funders **do not** exchange this increased accountability with increased flexibility. They do not give more discretion in the use of authority. They don't allow the flexibility to make  informed decisions about the resources and inputs used, the outputs to produce, and the way they are produced. They ask for banana bread but don't trust the organization to figure out how to make it, even if they are a professional bakery.

Too often, the funder ALSO tells the employment professional EXACTLY how to do it:

- Here are the workshops to be delivered, with ALL of the curriculum, handouts, exercises, tests, and methodologies.

- Here is the deficit-based, checklist-style needs assessment that MUST be used with all clients.

- Here is the decision model that outlines the exact service interventions that MUST be provided if these prescribed client needs are present in the needs assessment.

- Here is the software that will determine if the job seeker is "job ready," with an action plan that MUST be used with each client (which is a series of dropdown boxes).

- Here is the decision model that MUST be used to determine which clients get wage subsidy and how much they should receive.

- Here is the client contact schedule that MUST be followed to ensure the client-practitioner relationship is maintained (there can only be a five percent lost-contact rate, so there MUST also be management sign-off if contact is lost with a client).

- Here is the case management system that MUST be used, which is very prescriptive and will place severe limitations on the therapeutic relationship.

- Here are the reams and reams of data that MUST be collected and uploaded monthly.

- Here is the exact model of how files MUST be managed and maintained.

- Here are the service standards that MUST be posted and adhered to.

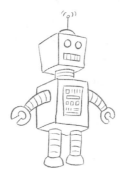

Although government funders are known to espouse "continuous improvement," "innovation," and "evidence-based practice," these buzzwords are curiously absent in the example above. The well trained, highly competent, sometimes professionally certified career development practitioner is reduced to an automated robot within a prescriptive GPS navigational system.

So, if you don't achieve the results, who is at fault? Can you be held accountable?

Well, this is a rhetorical question because regardless of how bastardized and convoluted the accountability relationship becomes, the funder DOES hold you accountable. If the above example rings a loud and familiar bell for you, it is likely that you are engaged in an "accountabalism" relationship with your funder.

In the 2007 *Harvard Business Review*, David Weinberger coined the term "accountabalism" and it rang bells for us, the authors. The imagery is compelling, turning an everyday corporate buzzword into a brain-eating zombie, slump-walking toward innovation and creativity, crushing values with yet another deficit-focused checklist, and eating brains. And, just like in B-movies, it can't be outrun.

Weinberger said: "Accountabalism turns complex problems into merely complicated systems, sacrificing innovation and adaptability."[13]

Governments want to avoid front page scandals, and they need those "Good News!" stories to replace those pages when scandals arise. According to Weinberger, governments look at

complex problems that have gone wrong for complex reasons, and they decide the problem can be solved at the next level of detail. Another set of guidelines and policies is written, and yet more forms are printed up. "When such disincentives as

the threat of having to wear an orange jumpsuit for eight to ten years didn't stop the Enron nightmare and other bad things from happening, 'accountabalism' whispered two seductive lies to us: Systems go wrong because of individuals; and the right set of controls will enable us to prevent individuals from creating disasters."[14] While claiming to increase individual responsibility, accountabalism drives out human judgment. Well said, Weinberger.

Not only does this mechanization not work (and you know it), it also takes the "fun" out of our "functional" work (and you know that too). It leads to disengagement, where employees have lost their joie de vivre and go from being emotionally engaged in their work (*How can I help and go the extra mile?*) to rationally engaged (*Just tell me what to do and I'll do it . . . maybe*). Forcing morality through administration or automating

13 David Weinberger, "The Folly of Accountabalism," *Harvard Business Review,* February 2007, 54.

14 David Weinberger, "The Folly of Accountabalism," *Harvard Business Review,* February 2007, 54.

processes in an attempt to solve complex problems reduces staff capacity to the very lowest common denominator, not the highest. Innovative, reflective, purposeful practitioners cannot operate in this restrictive environment, so they leave. Their abandoned caseloads and performance statistics become someone else's problem. Imagine how hard it would be to start a new job in this environment while also trying desperately to establish trust relationships with clients who were already feeling extremely discouraged. There goes that lower-than-five-percent lost-contact rate target . . .

It then becomes a perpetual, dysfunctional conga line. Funders issue contracts with hard targets that sound good to the taxpayer in media announcements but have little to do with quality outcomes for the "right" people, achieved through sound, evidence-based practice. These contracts are backed up by volumes of prescriptive evaluation and audit guidelines that are rarely risk-based, shackling the government program manager and creating a power-over relationship based on fear of failure and withdrawal of funding.

FUNDER   MANAGER   EMPLOYMENT   JOB   EMPLOYER
                     COUNSELLOR   DEVELOPER

Here's the conga line: the service provider's managers drive this flawed performance framework down to the staff level, driving out human judgment and innovation while automating the client–practitioner relationship. As the targets get harder to achieve, more energy is put into dubious practices that make it look like results are being achieved while clients with the highest needs (the MOONS and CLOUDS) are left behind. Staff morale can fall into a perpetual tailspin, which is another dance altogether.

This is not success.

Career development practitioners are left figuring out how to achieve targets no matter what, within a system riddled with controls, because they like feeding their children and paying their mortgage.

CAUSE #3: ONLY WINNERS GET ELECTED!

Risk-Averse Governments Don't Make Tough Decisions

"I promise that, if elected, poor unemployed people will remain poor and unemployed," said no one, ever.

Because employment touches every aspect of our lives, employment (and unemployment) is always a highly charged, top priority political issue. As the number one solution to issues around crime, poverty, family stability, and the economy, employment is predominant in most election platforms and budget speeches.

As a result, governments really dislike pulling funding from an employment agency. Who needs that kind of front-page coverage? How can the government  say they believe in strong economies and employment for all but then defund the programs or agencies that are supposed to help people secure employment?

And because a **lot** of money gets moved around with these programs (oodles of millions), funders are also cautious to avoid appearances that they are giving favour to any one agency or any one type of service provider: profit versus non-profit, community-based, school boards, or post-secondary programs. They want to appear "fair."

Avoiding tough decisions can pose significant challenges for the delivery of effective employment programs.

Some communities have ended up with too many employment service providers within a small geographic area. There are communities where the same government program is being run by seven different agencies within a ten-block radius. Or, there is one agency on the first floor and one on the third floor of the same office tower. Or, one on the east side and one on the west side of the same shopping mall. In all of these scenarios, these agencies are held to outcome-based contracts, where their funding is dependent upon opening and closing a set number of clients files, allocating a set amount of subsidy dollars to employers, and achieving quantifiable positive results.

In all of these scenarios, these agencies compete for the same clients and the same employers, and their budget stability depends on them winning. Despite the guideline requirements for "community collaboration," "no wrong door," and "local labour market planning," competition is necessary for survival and results in cutthroat practices (aka **Bullsh*t Survival Practices**). A saturated, highly competitive market often destabilizes the very behaviour of a community. The funded footprint is all wrong, and EVERYONE knows it, but the tough decisions are avoided by funders year over year.

Yet other communities, often smaller and remote, are grossly underserved. Safely cocooned as the only funded employment agency in town, the small community organization faces no competition. The risk here is there being so many clients to serve that "creaming" becomes as easy as plucking cherries from a bowl. And the few local, small-town employers ONLY hire through that agency, as they are guaranteed wage subsidies or other human resource perks. In these circumstances, so-called "marginal" clients are often left behind, as targets will more easily be achieved without them. The funded footprint of service delivery agencies is all wrong, again.

Sometimes, it is not about the funded footprint. Sometimes, agencies essentially become untouchable. In many communities, the employment programs are run by non-profit organizations that provide other "hub" services, such as food banks, literacy, settlement, education, and health programs. These agencies can be highly embedded within a community and very publicly visible in their lobbying and advocacy efforts. Often, these hub models of community service delivery are very efficient and customer focused. Some agencies enjoy a status of being "untouchable," so cutting their funding could be political ruin, even if the agency is failing to meet basic performance outcomes in employment services. We, in our dealings with funders and service providers, have seen some agencies receive performance improvement letters ("smarten up or you're out") for three consecutive years from the government and they are still not out, despite strong evidence of really poor performance, at best. Imagine yourself in the position of a down-and-out job seeker, hanging your hopes (and those of your family) on those funded agencies.

Sadly, this sometimes means agencies that SHOULD lose their funding due to consistent failed performance do not. Even though the consequences are clearly stated in the service contract, tough funding decisions may be avoided for political gain.

When avoiding tough decisions becomes endemic, it ends up with a service delivery network at odds with itself, and fiddling around the edges will no longer clean up the mess. One can eventually expect a wholesale, earth-shattering government program change where the baby is thrown out with the bathwater.

CAUSE #4: SAME OL' EMPLOYMENT PROGRAM DESIGN

Whenever we cautiously optimistic authors learn that a new government-funded employment program is in the works, we speculate about whether this new-fangled program will address the flaws revealed in the one or more previous program(s). We listen intently as the government speaks of current research and proven "best practices" in employment service design. Oh boy, we get sooo excited. We are truly hopeful

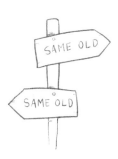

that something fresh and new is on the horizon. Once the program is announced, we pore over the guidelines, then call each other to say, "Dang. Same program, different name." Typically, it's a "teach-a-job-seeker-how-to-fish" model, so they will (fingers crossed) fish for a lifetime.

In our combined six decades of experience, "new" employment service programs—even when presented differently—are almost always based on the traditional job-readiness model. This model aims to identify and fix job seeker deficiencies and then support them to land their own jobs. Job seekers are asked to identify two to three of their *dream jobs*, chosen from about 30,000 National Occupational Codes (NOC) job titles that are classified in 500-unit groups (we're not kidding). They are taught how to write resumes and cover letters for those jobs (*backspace, backspace, enter, enter, control C, control V . . .*), how to interview *(If you were a utensil, which utensil would you be?)*, how to network and make a cold call, how to impress the pants off an employer and land the job. See? Easy peasy lemon squeezy!

This model **can** work BRILLIANTLY for job seekers who could have fished on their own in the first place: the STARS and SUNS. Sometimes.

If a job seeker isn't successful landing a job in this traditional model, it may be assumed that it is the job seeker's fault—they are just not doing it right. So, the prac-

titioner reviews the resume (*All together now, ONE more TIME!*) and conducts additional mock interviews (*Remember to smile, lean in, and nod*) and signs the job seeker up for more workshops (*How about we try the mock interview bootcamp?*). When the job seeker is frustrated by this process and gives up, their lack of effort and success is seen as evidence that they just did not try hard enough (*See? They weren't motivated anyway!*). An age-old *systemic* problem is treated as a problem with the client. Even worse, the client may blame themselves for the poor outcome, naive about that fact that they never stood a chance with the type of support that was provided in the first place.

The formulaic methodology of the traditional job-readiness model works fairly reliably for a very small percentage of people—the STARS and the SUNS. They have

the skills and experience, and **none or few employer perception barriers**, so they are taught to fish and they are on their way. There is much fanfare and back patting when this job seeker lands a job. They were taught to fish and they caught fish! (*Yay us!*) This is also a simple model for employment counsellors, as it is pretty transactional, prescriptive, and predictable. There is no need for in-depth counselling models to understand or address resistance, motivation issues, and life stability factors.

  Unfortunately, this model **DOES NOT WORK FOR THE MOONS** and **CLOUDS**, the people these programs are typically targeted to serve (yes, yelling intended). This is because two key areas are missing from the traditional model:

1.   Addressing the lack of motivation to work; and/or

2.   Influencing and supporting employers to hire from a non-traditional pool of job seekers

The **traditional job-readiness model** is built for "traditional" job seekers. In this model, the vast majority of program resources are focused on *building a better job seeker*, yet the majority of job seekers who are "locked out" of the market are locked out because of **market perception issues, not because of poor job-search skills. They are locked out BECAUSE they are "non-traditional"; they don't fit employers' mental models of the ideal employee.** These con-  scious or unconscious biases ensure that these job seekers cannot compete, or are not welcome to compete (they may be invited to the party, but not asked to dance). It is  unfathomable that these job seekers are made to compete using traditional methods, then they are blamed for being unemployed, then labelled as being "not motivated." The reality is, they've hit their heads against the wall so many times, with so many doors closed—including the employment service's—that they have just given up. They just don't have the strength to knock on the door anymore.

Under the job-readiness model, every job seeker is trained and then expected to become proficient self-marketers, in a very short period of time. The most important outcome measure for employment agencies is the bottom line: landing a job for a specified number of clients. Yet the job-readiness model places the critical function of "closing the deal" on the backs of job seekers—the least experienced, least resourceful, most discriminated-against people . . . which then puts the organization's reputation and funding at risk because it consistently does not work.

There is a general expectation that job seekers must win competitions to get a job. Yet lots of people secure jobs *without* winning competitions. Don't believe us? Think about your first job. Did you have the skills to do that job when you applied for it? Did you land it on your own or did someone land it for you? Would your mother/father/caregiver have said you were "job ready"?

Ask any hiring manager and they will tell you that resumes and interviews are REALLY poor predictors of success on the job. If a finely crafted resume and the ability to "act" during an interview was all that was needed for long term success, companies would not need human resource departments and progressive discipline.

Once a "new" employment service program is implemented, it doesn't take long for "gaming" and "creaming" to start, even if the program is a "pilot." It's the same old, same old . . .

How much more research and data are needed to demonstrate that the traditional job-readiness model does not work for the MOONS and CLOUDS—those most distant from the labour market? *"But employers want the STARS and SUNS,"* you say. Truth is, STARS and SUNS can turn out to be MOONS and CLOUDS, and vice versa. Neither you nor the employer can predict, based on a resume or an interview, if someone will work out on a job. In fact, some companies have successfully eliminated the resume and interview process completely, through a process called "Open Hiring." The first person to show up, gets the job.[15] Hiring is a crapshoot—always—even with the fanciest employee selection tools.

We know (and so do you) that the traditional ways employment services are delivered often leave job  seekers, and even employers, without the services they seek and deserve. It's time to look at this challenge with a different lens.

---

15 David DeLong and Sara Marcus, "Imagine a Hiring Process Without Resumes," *Harvard Business Review,* January 5, 2021, https://hbr.org/2021/01/imagine-a-hiring-process-without-resumes.

CAUSE #5: LACK OF SERVICE PROVIDER CAPACITY

Here is a real-life story to demonstrate what a systemic lack of capacity to deliver employment services for the MOONS and CLOUDS looks like in practice. Not even a little bit of  this is made up, but we have omitted the name of the program itself (and let's not kid ourselves that this only happened once).

A few years ago, a new employment program for "marginalized," disengaged youth was launched. This government program used policy and performance measures to direct employment service providers to work with youth who were the MOST disengaged, often CLOUDS.

The program serves youth aged 15 to 29 who experience multiple and/or complex barriers to employment by providing more intensive support beyond traditional job search and placement opportunities.

To ensure the intended job seekers were served (the "very marginalized"), the program had a "suitability factor." The funder provided a list of complex barriers and required that each participating job seeker, *on average*, had 35 percent of these indicators, which worked out to about 3.85 indicators per person. Here they are:

1. Indigenous Person

2. Person with disability

3. Under 20 years of age

4. Recent immigrant (less than five years in the country)

5. Grade 12 or less

6. Language barrier

7. Low level of proficiency in one or more of nine essential skills

8. Poor/no work experience

9. Unstable family household situation (low-income household, little/no parental involvement, acts as primary caregiver or lone head of household, lives alone with no/low income)

10. Socially marginalized (homeless, LGBTTQ+, addiction, criminal involvement, crown ward/child welfare system)

11. Source of income (welfare, employment insurance, disability benefit, no income, etc.)

Pick any three or four of these indicators, and you have a "hard to serve" youth. Add indicators 9 or 10, and service delivery becomes downright complex, bordering on the provision of clinical counselling.

One would be hard pressed to argue against the need for this type of career development program for disengaged youth. In fact, we believe that this is an extremely important program—here's the evidence-based reason for this:

- Lack of education and job training significantly lowers an individual's lifetime earnings.

- One single disengaged youth (Not in Employment, Education or Training [NEET]) places an estimated burden of $704,020 (USD) on society over their entire lifetime.

- Youth aged 16–19 face the highest rate of unemployment of all age groups. There is a very high risk that

disengaged youth will eventually fail to become productive adults.[16]

The research goes on to say that disengaged youth are also more likely to be living in poverty, receiving public assistance, incarcerated, homeless, on death row (US), unhealthy, divorced, single parents, and, ultimately, high school dropouts with children who drop out from high school themselves.[17] So engaging youth into education, employment, or both is a worthy outcome.

Research highlights three required components for an effective career development program for disengaged youth.[18] Let's compare it to the youth program mentioned above:

1. **Applied Skills Development** that provides youth with relevant hard and soft skills.

    ✓ **Check.** The program has 60–90 hours of pre-employment learning and training. Employment organizations have FULL flexibility on how they  design their syllabus, how, when, and where they deliver the training. Youth are paid minimum wage

---

16   Kate Hanley, et al., *Youth Career Development Social Issue Report* (Root Cause, April 2012), 2, https://rootcause.org/wp-content/uploads/2019/05/Youth-Career-Development-Social-Issue-Report.pdf.

17   Ibid.

18   Ibid.

to attend. The service providers are the experts; they decide what and how to teach.

2. **Career Exposure** that improves youths' understanding of career opportunities, which can lead to a family-sustaining wage.

    ✓ **Check.** The program has a mandatory job placement component. Employers receive an incentive to create a career exposure opportunity for the youth. Employment organizations have full discretion on the how long, where, and how. Three-week, full-time placement? *Sure.* One-day job trial? *Yep.* One-week employer assessment? *No problem.* Up to you, experts. Whichever best fits the unique needs of your youth.

3. Youth **Development Services** to help at-risk and in-risk youth address and overcome their individual barriers to success.

    ✓ **Check.** The Service Planning and Coordination component of the program IS case management, including needs assessment, goal setting and action planning, managed and supported referrals to external supports to deal with stability factors and move the plan forward, ongoing coaching, evaluation, etc.

Sounds like a good program, no? It seems to address critical job seeker needs AND the program design lines up with recognized best practice research. Bonus points for the high levels of flexibility on HOW the agency *chooses* to deliver the program, meeting the rules of modern accountability. What could possibly go wrong?

Well, *everything*. Unfortunately, despite solid program design and the best of intentions, the program did not have the desired result.

By mid-2017, in their efforts to determine the nature of the problem, the funder held roundtable discussions to determine what was wrong. **The program was failing miserably.** Service providers were unable to hit their exit targets, even when more than enough youth signed up for and started participating in the program. Job placements were not happening, and when they were, the success rates were very poor. There was very little evidence of referrals to community partners for support, even though there was ample evidence of marginalization and need. While the service provider network recognized that re-engagement with education had the potential to be the most successful outcome for these youth, MOST of the program outcomes (around 65 percent) were in part-time, precarious, minimum-wage jobs with no future. At the six-month mark, many of these employment outcomes had failed. Far fewer than 10 percent of youth were re-engaged in education.

At the round tables, at conferences, and in letters to the funder, service providers cried "foul." From their perspective, the policy needed to be revamped. They said they were failing because of program design.

But here's the catch.

This program gave the service providers INCREDIBLE flexibility with respect to HOW to design and implement their program.

As consultants, the authors were hired to help improve the program. So, we got into the weeds, waded through the swamp, and looked under the micro- scope. Here is a summary of what we observed,  across the board (while we noted a few excellent practices, they were not the norm):

1. Formal, traditional, instructor-led training, largely in-class, based on class cohort, mimicking the educational system that did not work for the youth the first time around.

2. Syllabi for the 60–90 hours of learning and training, if the program facilitator was able to produce them, were simply glorified job-readiness clubs. The first few hours were typically dedicated to writing resumes (*Pray tell, what will their resumes hold? Not much or nada or zilch*), and much of the remainder focused on teaching the youth how to fish in a competitive market. It was very SUPPLY-FOCUSED to build a better job seeker.

3. Reflecting on the **dozens** of agencies that we visited, NOT ONE program created short-, medium-, and

long-term action plans with the youth. NOT ONE. There was no focus on future planning, no identification of strengths, no evidence of creating hopefulness through a vision of a preferred future. And since there was no discussion about where the youth wanted to be in 10 years, there was no discussion of pathways to get there, and, therefore, no conversation about education or training options.

4. We saw employment counsellors that were not trained to provide counselling. We met with workshop facilitators with little knowledge about pedagogy and alternative learning principles. We saw job developers who had neither the confidence nor the experience to work with employers. Case management was viewed as an administrative function. We saw the most marginalized, at-risk youth being put in the care of career development "professionals" who appeared to be mostly glorified resume writers in a supply-focused job-readiness model.

The program success rates and lost-contact rates made it clear. Not only was the program failing to assist the youth, the youth were being re-traumatized by a formal system that was completely unresponsive to their unique needs and circumstances. And instead of looking inward, many agencies adopted a victim mentality and placed the blame on policy, on clients they perceived to be unmotivated, on inflexible employers, and on a poor labour market. *Ouch!*

The problem, as we saw it, was simple. Many of the agencies contracted to run the program clearly lacked the capacity to do it. Why?

a. **Lack of Capacity—No Professional Standards:** In most jurisdictions, there are no professional standards required to be a career development practitioner professional. National Professional Standards[19] exist in Canada (and around the world), but they are usually not mandatory, and if they are, there are no systems in place to ensure they are practised and perfected, such as clinical supervision. ANYONE can call themselves an employment counsellor, without even a stitch of formal counselling or career development education or experience or supervision. Government funders worldwide pour billions of dollars into employment programs with the genuine intention of trying to solve a desperate employment situation for those most marginalized, through a network that is often lacking the most basic skills required to do the job. Staff don't have a professional practice; instead, they have targets to meet, papers to push, money to spend, and statistics to compile.

b. **Lack of Capacity—Process Burden:** Unnecessary and unhelpful prescriptive paperwork drives out good practice, or low-value but mandatory activities leave no space for authentic work. The message is clear in the employment service industry: *Just get the numbers and spend the money and don't ask any questions.*

---

19   The Canadian Standards & Guidelines for Career Development Practitioners, 2001, https: career-dev-guidelines.org.

c. **Lack of Capacity—Low Wages:** Low wages in traditional non-profit settings don't help the situation. Agencies may be challenged to attract a skilled, motivated workforce  with the wages they are able to offer. The sad but honest truth is that there is sometimes a perception that employment counselling is what one does when one can't find a real counselling job. *Ouch!*

d. **Lack of Capacity—Poor Leadership:** Management may struggle to understand what competencies are needed, they may measure the wrong things, and they may lack basic training and supervision. There may be little in the way of team learning and reflective practice. They are often promoted from a front-line job and not taught how to lead and  manage people and things. But can management be blamed, given the struggles they themselves face? Everyone has a little egg on their face.

e. **Lack of Capacity—Cookie Cutter Programming:** Regardless of the program design or intent, some agencies have tended to respond to clients' needs by responding with what can only be described as assembly-line program delivery: every job seeker gets the same services and the same interventions. One size fits ... well, 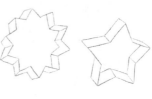 maybe for the SUNS and STARS. It is usually supply-focused, even though they are working predominantly with MOONS and CLOUDS (or should be).

f. **Lack of Capacity—Transactional Energy Leaks:** In the absence of reflective and responsive practice, we see energy leaks through busy-work and make-work projects, such as running workshops with empty chairs, holding job fairs that are built for the STARS and SUNS, writing resumes (even though the resume can't compete), and pro-  viding employer subsidies that leave the marginalized behind. *Take a number—your number is zero.*

g. **Lack of Capacity—Access to the Hidden Job Market:** Service providers have a very small roster of employers who consider them to be credible, trusted sources for job candidates, and, therefore, they do not know, or have access to, the wide range of jobs that are filled through referrals—the unpublished, less competitive, hidden job market. This leads to a severe lack of under-standing of the immediate and longer-term needs of the local labour market, the *micro* labour market, the pain points that keep employers up at night. These needs can only be revealed by actually talking to lots and lots of employ- 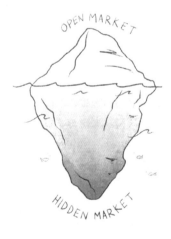 ers, directly and frequently. Job developers, some of whom really just want to work 1-to-1 with clients, are terrified to reach out to employers—so they work with a small roster of employers who reach out to them often with jobs they can't fill (*Hello low-wage, precarious, revolving-door jobs*). They also chase published, open-market jobs (a small percentage of available jobs), which leaves clients competing (or not) with other, more qualified candidates.

Over-selling and under-delivering the service to employers is a key reason why employers don't work with service providers. Here's how this plays out:

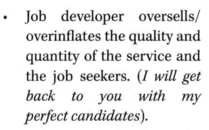

- Job developer finds a public job posting.

- Job developer asks the employer for the "wish list of features" of their ideal candidate. (*What are the qualities you are looking for in a perfect candidate?*)

- Job developer oversells/overinflates the quality and quantity of the service and the job seekers. (*I will get back to you with my perfect candidates*).

- Job developer inundates the employer with resumes that don't match the employer's wish list requirements. (*Please find 10 resumes attached and get back to me*).

When the employer ghosts the job developer (*They said they wanted to hire but won't return my calls, after I emailed them 10 resumes*), the job developer blames the poor quality of the resumes and job seekers, rather than their own inability to build relationships with employers to understand their real needs, to overcome employer objections, and to deliver a *good enough* employee. (Spoiler alert: *most* employees are good enough/average performers.)

The role of employment services is to prepare people for, and connect people to, sustainable employment in their communities. This means you have to actually talk to employers (*what a concept!*). If employers like, trust, and respect you, it's possible to build long  term, mutually beneficial, reciprocal relationships that open up opportunities for job seekers who would have been overlooked.

h. **Lack of Capacity—Business Intelligence:** Service providers and governments alike often suffer from low *business intelligence*—they don't know what data/evidence to collect, how to collect it with integrity, where to find it, how to analyse it, what it is telling them, and how to use it to improve their service. This trickles down to front-line staff who often have no idea what the contracted commitments are, and therefore how their performance compares. They are often surprised and angry when they hear they've been celebrating reaching a fraction of their contracted targets.

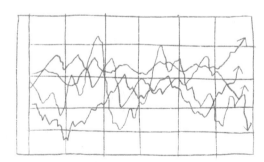

The youth program highlighted is just one story of many that demonstrates the potential impact when service providers lack the capacity to deliver the fundamental basics of a responsive, effective, needs-based employment service, whatever the demographic.

CAUSE #6: MYTHS AND MINDSETS

Often, people with employment barriers are unemployed due to employer myths and mindsets, the "isms": racism, sexism, ableism, ageism, etc. Government programs marketing sound bites perpetuate these myths and mindsets, for example, *"xyz program acts as a link to help people with disabilities gain training and experience to confidently step into open employment."* Well-meaning employment professionals reinforce the myths and mindsets when they present the profile of these job seekers to employers as people with complex employment barriers. (*Good News! She comes with a wage subsidy!*). Often facing discrimination, these job seekers can be hard-pressed to compete against other applicants, especially if those applicants are recently unemployed or currently working and looking for a new job. Often, this lack of success is internalized as yet another personal failure.

Job seekers with *employer perception barriers* ("isms") need someone to break into the labour market with them or for them. That is supposed to be the role of the funded employment program, but too often these programs may themselves be part of the problem. Again, achieving the contracted outcomes for "hard-to-serve" job seekers is seen as an impossibility for agencies in survival mode. And we agree—it IS impossible, if they are using the same poor practices and expecting better results. Too often, the struggling organization and its staff work under the "give a person a fish and you feed them for a day; teach a person to fish and you feed them for a lifetime" mentality. "Throw them a fish" is firmly against their philosophical model. Instead, they focus exclusively on how to build a better job seeker, teaching the skills and competencies to find, win, perform, and keep a job. *Make the client shiny and employers will hire them.*

But here's the rub: there are no employment skills workshops that will make a job seeker less disabled, less female, younger, and white. You can put them through weeks and weeks of your job seeker bootcamp, and they are still facing ableism, sexism, ageism, and racism. You can teach them to fish for the next three years, but employers still won't let them anywhere near the pond. And when these "hard-to-serve" job seekers become discouraged and surrender, they become a negative statistic and are often blamed for being resistant, unmotivated, and lazy. *Ouch!*

You see, when there are *structural, systemic* barriers to employment, the client with employment barriers who wants to work and is not working should not be identified as the problem. The problem is the employer. The flaw in the "teach to fish" strategy is that it is focused only on the supply side of the employment equation, enhancing the skills of the job seeker. For the employment "supply chain" to function effectively, the demand side (employers) of the equation needs to be both engaged and influenced by the agency. And this takes a lot more than a shiny program brochure and gifts of free, program-branded tote bags, baseball hats, and key rings, which become landfill, exacerbating another serious problem.

If you have job seekers "stuck in the hopper," sitting on your caseload, messing up your agency's performance statistics, maybe the solution is not to build a better job seeker. Perhaps it is to build better (and more) employer relationships.

EXERCISE: TIME OUT
FOR REFLECTION

Which of these causes resonate with you (if any)?

_____

_____

_____

_____

What causes have not been mentioned?

_____

_____

_____

_____

CHAPTER 5:

Virtuous Thrivival Principles

CHAPTER 5:

Virtuous Thrivival Principles

W OULDN'T IT BE wonderful if this were one of those high school textbooks where the answer key was at the back? (What were they thinking?)

We know the employment problem is worth fixing.

Unemployment in general, *and systemic unemployment in particular,* has a tremendous cost. Governments are spending billions of dollars on employment programming, yet those populations most in need are still largely being left behind, costing billions of dollars in human and societal ills.

But truth be told, if there were a simple solution, it would have been implemented long ago.

- There is no well-designed performance measurement framework that will pull everyone in line.

- There is no single political party promise.

- No amount of government funding.

- No magical program design.

- No scathing auditor's report.

- No solution-focused training program.

- No agency certification program.

- No service quality model.

- No single policy fix.

But there are changes, some of them small, that could be made in several areas that would make a big difference. We know that everyone in the sector has ideas and experience to bring to the table, to help make this better, even just a little bit.

In this chapter, we are going to share the key things that we believe are necessary for "thrivival." Not just surviving in tough, outcome-based funding models, but **thriving**. These fall under three categories:

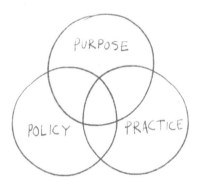

These areas cannot be dealt with in isolation, as they are part of an interconnected system. When one area falls, it brings everything down with it.

We believe meaningful transformation in the employment service sector starts with the end in mind. It starts with Purpose.

PURPOSE

If a government funder, agency manager, employment counsellor, or job developer does not understand their purpose, or if they lose touch with their purpose, then policy and practice do not much matter.

In fact, **nothing else matters.** Your purpose is what gets you out of bed in the morning, it drives you to perform with integrity, gives you the courage to speak truth to power, fuels your desire to seek solutions and solve problems. Your conviction to purpose would have you choose to be unemployed yourself rather than gaming a system that leaves families in poverty while giving out wage subsidies to people who would have been hired anyway. It is understanding the hypocrisy of your stable employment on the backs of those who need your service the most. The employment sector IS a passion and purpose sector. No practitioner is in this field to get rich.

Here are some key thrivial concepts to consider in **Purpose**:

1. **Reconnect with your purpose, or get out.**

   We hope you are in it for purpose. And if you are not, it is possible you are part of the problem. Find a way to reconnect to the purpose of your job, your vision/mission/mandate, the reason you exist. Or get out and get work that aligns with your purpose.

2. **Tether EVERYTHING to Purpose.**

   Government funder, managers, and executive directors, it is YOUR JOB to wave the purpose flag continuously and enthusiastically. To plant that flag firmly in the ground, and tether everything to it.

Note that what you measure **is what you VALUE.**

Take a moment, and jot down the top five things that you measure.

So, what do you measure?

_____

_____

_____

Really—what do you measure?

_____

_____

_____

How do those things drive behaviours? Toward your purpose, or away from it?

Build your purpose into your hiring processes, your performance evaluations, your performance frameworks, your weekly meetings. Make your purpose CENTRAL in your strategic plans, your operational plans, your decision frameworks. Acknowledge and reward practices that align with your purpose and nip the rotten ones in the bud. Make partnerships that move your purpose forward, not partnerships that spend your money quickly.

3. **Use your Purpose Power wisely.**

    Governments are the stewards of the public purse AND the people. If you are an elected official, you were granted power by the majority, who believed in you to do right by them. If you are a civil servant, you hold one of the best paid and most secure jobs available. Through the public purse, you wield power to design, adhere to, and achieve your stated purpose. (Hint: Your purpose is not to guarantee the re-election of your current government.) Use your purpose power wisely.

Solving this employment problem STARTS with all players in the system being firmly anchored in purpose, whether you are governments designing and funding employment programs, agencies delivering these programs, or practitioners on the front lines. Take the time to figure out why you exist, what problem you are trying to solve, and then NEVER lose sight of it. Be brave. Tell the truth (it will set you free). Whole populations of people are depending on you.

TIME OUT FOR AN EXERCISE

Reflect on your purpose.

How did you end up in the field of employ-ment services? As a dreamy seven-year-old, did you come home from public school with the hand-drawn poster of conviction that read: "When I grow up, I want to be an employment counsellor"? We didn't think so.

Take five minutes to answer these questions:

Why are you in this field?

_____

_____

_____

_____

What brought you here?

_____

_____

_____

_____

What keeps you here?

_____

_____

_____

_____

How will the world be better because of you?

_____

_____

_____

_____

Did you struggle to answer these questions, or did they flow from you with passion and poetry?

People often fall into this field, and they get their business cards printed before they even really get what the job is all about. Once they know, they see the potential for great things—to make a difference in the lives of others. Use that power wisely.

POLICY

Governments, you set the stage for effective, purposeful practice. Your program guidelines become the *Bible of Program Behaviour.*

If you tell me I must, I will. If you tell me I must not, I won't. If you leave it grey (like "should" or other fuzzities), I will look for clues to make best guesses on the choices I think you MOST want me to make.

Because you hold the purse strings.

Governments, don't underestimate the impact your program policy and program design have on the ultimate outcomes that are achieved.

Here are some key thrivival concepts to consider in **Policy:**

1. **Figure out your purpose.** Re-read the Purpose section, do the exercises.

2. **Figure out who you serve.** Hint: public servants.

3. **Speak truth to power, pick your hard.**

   Find a way to meet the desires (these are not actual needs) of your reigning government party WHILE building lasting, effective, evidence-based program policy. This means speaking truth to power to honour both your purpose and the public to whom you are a servant. **This is hard.**

Or, roll out a poorly designed, election-promise program that you know will fail, and face scathing auditor general reports, media scrutiny, non-profit sector resentment, long term labour market issues, poor economic development, and blame by the next government. **This is also hard.**

Pick your hard.

4. **Only roll out evidence-based employment programming.** You've done the research, paid for program evaluations, and reviewed the interjurisdictional findings of other countries trying to solve these problems. None of this is new.

- Wage subsidies fail marginalized populations.

- The traditional job-readiness model fails marginalized populations. Stop focusing so heavily on polishing the supply-side (more resumes and job clubs!) and roll out programs that actually deliver outcomes for marginalized populations. This is true job development (not job orders, job matching, etc.).

- The people who deliver employment programs on the ground, every day, have wisdom and experience to share to improve services. They are the face of your programs, and no one is closer to the job seekers and employers. **No one.** Ignore them at your peril.

- Policy and programs need to be executed by competent career development professionals, with effective, empowering tools and technologies. How a practitioner chooses to practice matters. Invest in their competence.

5. **Bullsh*t Performance Measurement Frameworks** generate **Bullsh*t Survival Practices.**

If you build punitive performance-measurement frameworks that measure simple, consumable political sound bites instead of the intended purpose, don't be surprised if practice on the ground becomes wildly unhinged. What you measure communicates what you value. And what you value gets done, oh Mighty Purse String Holder. (Remember, YOUR program policy and guidelines are the Bible of Behaviour.)

6. **Stop hog-tying your service delivery network.**

The rules of accountability dictate that outcome-based accountability must be exchanged for greater flexibility. Stop hog-tying your service delivery network with unnecessary and burdensome rules and regulations.

Stop removing all of their professional autonomy with automated systems and dropdown lists that:

- Assume all clients fit into the same boxes.

- Demoralize and decrease client hopefulness.

- Kill the therapeutic alliance or client–practitioner relationship. And,

- Remove all professional discretion in career development and motivational techniques.

Governments entrust billions of dollars to these career development professionals. They are expected to solve complex problems. Build programs that respect this fact.

PRACTICE

After years of yoga, it struck us how often the yogi talked about our yoga "practice"—investing in it, knowing what we want to get out of it, etc.

We have never, ever, in the decades that we have been in the field, heard employment counsellors and job developers talk about their "practices." And we believe that needs to change.

In their book *Peak*, Ericsson and Pool describe what they call "purposeful practice" and its four essential components: [20]

1. Purposeful practice has well-defined, specific goals and vision.

    If you don't have clear values or vision of expertise, your practice is unlikely to be effective. *What do you believe in?*

2. Purposeful practice is focused.

    Practice *should* be hard.

3. Purposeful practice involves feedback.

    You can't watch yourself swing.

4. Purposeful practice requires getting out of one's comfort zone.

    Magic does not happen in your comfort zone.

---

20 Anders Ericsson, Robert Pool, *Peak: Secrets from the New Science of Expertise* (Boston: Eamon Dolan/HMH 2016), 15–17.

Nothing in employment service delivery gets done without people, and you are the people to get it done. Billions of tax dollars are funnelled to service delivery agencies to solve complex social and labour market challenges.

The career development "practitioners" are the foot soldiers. You are the "case managers" of caseloads of thousands of humans that want and need a better future. It's up to you whether you want to window dress to make it look like you are delivering brilliant services or to really deliver them, which can be pretty ugly and messy at times. It's always a choice.

The moment you hear yourself saying you would LOVE to serve people with employment barriers but can't because your funder is making you just hit the numbers and spend the money, is the moment you might want to move on. Because then you are not only part of the problem, you ARE the problem. You have lost touch with both your purpose and your practice.

In a purposeful practice, here are some key thrivival concepts to consider:

1. **Know what you signed up for.**

    Your customers are the MOONS and CLOUDS, **not** just the SUNS and STARS. Without them and their needs, your service would not exist. These people are not "broken," they do not need to be "fixed." Focus on their strengths, not their deficits. Believe that your job seekers are creative, resourceful, and whole, as are you. Your genuine belief in this will be the foundation of your practice. Remember:

    - It is about their needs, not yours.

    - Their path, not yours.

    - Give them the benefit of the doubt, then give them a chance. And another, if need be (and another).

    - Be responsive. Many job seekers are desperate, and their needs fall on the lowest tiers of *Maslow's Hierarchy of Needs*. It may not be urgent for you, but it is for them.

    - They are human—remember their humanness.

- Meet them where they are at and walk with them. The only thing that separates you from your job seekers is employment.

Keep this human at the centre of the system, as they are the primary customer. They came to the program to help them find solutions to potentially crippling issues. When the service engages them, that engagement brings great accountability. Their future is determined by what these programs do. Everyone has a role to play in the accountability relationship. Don't fug around with that.

Identifying client needs, selecting the right combination of end-to-end services, and strong employer relationships allows organizations to deliver on results promised to attract and effectively serve funders, clients, and employers, which will benefit the community as a whole.

This is what you signed up for.

2. **Commit to a culture of right action.**

"If a professional is faced with a decision to do the right thing, even when it costs them, that's the price of being a professional. That's what being a professional is all about, doing the right thing, even when there are powerful influences to do something else."[21]

---

21   J. Copeland, as referenced by Gloria A. Grizzle, "Performance Measurement and Dysfunction: The Dark Side of Quantifying Work," *Public Performance & Management Review* 24, no. 4 (2002):367, https://doi.org/10.1080/15309576.2002.11643673.

Fear creates poor practice. A culture of fear in the employment service industry leads to bad practice, where people feel like they are swimming through shark-infested waters; the lizard (survival) brain takes over.

There must be a steadfast commitment to right action, even when you lose. Right action is a choice. If everyone truly lived and operated using right action, from government to management to practitioners to employers, most of the problems discussed in this book would not exist. People need to PURPOSEFULLY create work environments that are conducive to right action. It doesn't just happen.

There isn't a right action playbook, but you know it when you see it.

Do the right thing.

3. **Hire the right people and engage their hearts.**

"People are not the most important asset in organizations, but the RIGHT people are."[22]

The hiring process is a golden opportunity to make sure you build a team of people that fits with your purpose. Think about your interview process. Do ANY of your questions actually assess purpose and right action? What evidence do you see during your interview process of people guided by purpose, moral code, and a drive to do better? The questions you ask set the early foundation of what to expect from the culture of your organization.

The barriers facing marginalized job seekers have deep roots and high walls, and these clients come to the

---

22 Jim Collins, *Good to Great* (New York: Harper Business, 2001), 13.

table as they are. You won't find solutions in a well-written resume. The right people have the understanding, skills, competencies, resources, and will to do the right thing within a complex system. Recognize the complexity of the field through your hiring process. Hire people with the education, skills, and experience to:

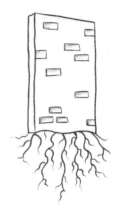

- Recognize and challenge systemic inequities.

- Help demoralized people find hope, inner motivation, and purpose.

- Be professional career development practitioners who respect their practice.

- Analyse and use local *micro* labour market information. And,

- Work with employers to identify business needs that can be addressed by the strengths of the employment service and its job seekers.

Hire a team that reflects the diversity of your community, as well as your commitment to equity and inclusion. This is not an act of charity; this is an act of having your service reflect the diversity of your community (repetition intended). Maybe your customers will come in the door without bribes if they feel like they are welcomed, valued, and understood.

Hiring the wrong people results in one hell of a mess. Get it right the first time.

Once you've got 'em, engage 'em. Their minds and their hearts.

Often the mostly actively disengaged employees were, at one time, actively engaged and incredibly motivated. At some point these employees switched from "How can I help?" to "Just tell me what to do and I'll do it (or at least make it look like I did)." How and when did THAT happen?

"The benefits of an engaged workforce are clear: increased productivity, decreased turnover, and improved business results. However, employee engagement has remained stubbornly low and relatively unchanged over decades."[23]

Employees who are emotionally engaged outperform those who are rationally engaged. Employees who are fully disengaged metaphorically quit their jobs a long time ago but are still collecting their paycheques. There are whole books dedicated to building emotionally engaged employees, and it is worth supporting and implementing employee-engagement strategies.

23 Colin Hall and Caitlin Comeau, *Employee Engagement: Driving Engagement From the Middle*. (Ottawa: Conference Board of Canada, 2018) https://www.conferenceboard.ca/e-library/abstract. aspx?did=9876 (accessed November 24, 2021)

Managers must make sure the right people are hired and, once they are hired, that they are doing the right things and are supported to be successful. This includes ensuring that basic psychological needs, such as autonomy, competency, and relatedness, are nurtured, as employees who tend to be emotionally engaged, motivated, productive, and content produce more favourable personal and organizational outcomes.[24]

And if you have staff who can't or won't do their jobs, get rid of them, even if it costs you. This is hard, but so is maintaining the illusion.

People who love their jobs love their clients and employers. People who don't love their jobs, don't.

> "If you take care of your employees, they'll take care of your customers." (Richard Branson)

4. **Define your operating model and your practice model.**

The journey from unemployment to employment is like a conveyor belt for some, and a treadmill for many. They eventually fly right off because they are out of breath and can't keep up; they are also going nowhere, fast. And we're not just talking about clients; we're talking about staff. They are often winging it as best they can because there is nothing for them to hold on to; they have no clearly defined model for their practice. They do what they are most comfortable doing

---

24 Dan H. Pink, *Drive: The Surprising Truth About What Motivates Us.* (Edinburg: Canongate, 2010).

(*wash-rinse-spin-repeat*) as do their colleagues
rinse-spin-repeat—but on a different setting).

A consistent operating model ensures that ever
knows how business is done in your centre. The m
is enshrined in policies and operating manuals, in
descriptions, in your staff onboarding, performan
reviews, and training plans. The model makes sure th
how, the when, the why, and the who of your operations
is crystal clear to all. It wouldn't matter which employment counsellor I saw, I would get consistent, high-quality
service in:

- Eligibility and suitability determination

- Assessment

- Planning

- Implementation and coordination

- Evaluation

- Follow-up

- Termination/transition

Now, that list is not meant to be prescriptive, but chances
are you can see your service delivery model in it. Essentially,
the pathway includes two parallel processes on the supply
(job seeker) and demand (employer) sides of the employment equation. The following is an example. Again, are
you and all your staff clear on the how, the when, the
why, and the who for each of the bubbles in **The Service
Pathway?** (see image on page 120). Because if you are not,
you are likely winging it. And while the laws of chaos say
you will have some success some of the time, consistent,
high-quality success most of the time is not likely.

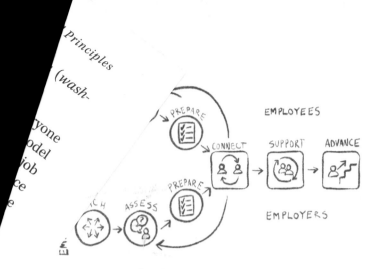

Principles
(wash-

yone
odel
job
ce
e

PREPARE

EMPLOYEES

CONNECT SUPPORT ADVANCE

PREPARE

RCH ASSESS PREPARE

EMPLOYERS

The Service Pathway

Identify the "energy leaks" (*Send more resumes!*) and "avoidance behaviours" (*Let's run another job fair!*) that happen when people are working outside the model, and address them.

Equally important to your operating models are your practice models.

The SAGE Encyclopedia of Theory in Counseling and Psychotherapy lists over 300 different approaches to counselling practice.[25]

Lucky for us, research says that one model is not more effective than another in achieving results. While your counselling technique is important, so is how you build relationships, how you build hopefulness, and how you uncover your clients' strengths and goals. Does your organization practice solution-focused brief therapy

25 E. S. Neukrug, ed., *The SAGE Encyclopedia of Theory in Counseling and Psychotherapy* (Thousand Oaks: Sage Publications, Inc., 2015).

approaches? Motivational interviewing? Cognitive-behavioural approaches? Do you know?

Because if you don't, there's a chance that your staff don't really know how to motivate behaviour change (regardless of how good their resume writing skills are).

The same applies to your job developers. What is their model? How do they approach sales? (And this IS sales.) Do you know what to look for in their model?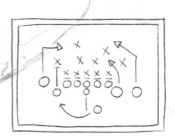

If you have not yet done so, define your operating and practice models. It is more important than you may think.

5. **Take employer engagement off of the side of the desk.**

Imagine you had so many great employer relationships, from a variety of sectors with a variety of jobs that match the interests and abilities of your job seekers. Imagine that when your job seekers are available for work, there is suitable work available for them.

Imagine if these employers trusted you and your recommendations so much that you didn't need to "close the sale" with a financial incentive, or a resume, or an interview.

Is this a pipe dream?

It is, if you are hoping by some miracle that the "right" employers will be beating down your door, asking for clients with employment barriers.

It isn't, if you have enough successful job developers who have more than enough employer partners who view them as trusted, credible business partners, working not only on behalf of the job seeker, but on behalf of the employer.

So, what happens instead? You fork over the responsibility for job development to the party you already know, dimes to doughnuts, will be the least successful: your clients. The vast majority of job seekers have never been trained in understanding the dynamics of the labour market, in structural inequities, in handling objections, in therapeutic approaches, in career theory, in career ethics, etc. The most marginalized clients have **NO IDEA** how to break into the market, and they usually do not have the tools, positional power, or resources to do so. And even if they did, it is not enough if employers won't even look at them in the first place (even if you gave the client a self-marketing letter).

Hopefully employees have been trained in real job development models, and hopefully those inform their practice. How a practitioner chooses to practice matters.

So, why don't you do job development when you know employers have crippling issues that need solving and they are also your customers? Are you afraid of the "NO"?

One big reason that employers say no to hiring your clients is because often they **perceive** that the costs of doing business with you (Yes, you!) outweigh the benefits. And if employers don't see your agency, or you, as credible, the issue is you, not your clients.

Employer engagement and job development can't be seen as an afterthought—something you do after everything else is done. It must be embedded in the employment service from end to end. This includes ensuring all team members, not just job developers, understand what job development is, who it is for, and how all team members can support clients before, during, and after employment. It requires that appropriate referrals are made to job development services and supports are provided once a client is on a job site.

To be a successful job developer, you must:

1. Get in touch with what is really happening in the *micro* labour market.

2. Take on the responsibility of shifting the mental models regarding marginalized populations. Don't trust that someone else is going to do this for you.

3. Do what you tell your clients to do. You tell them about the importance of networking with employers to access the hidden, unpublished, non-competitive market—but then you don't do it.

You need to consistently implement a process to find, serve, and keep employers, to be the first place they call when they have a job available. This planned approach will assist managers and job developers to understand the techniques that are working and those that fall short. It also helps to consistently assess individual and team performance and to build on strengths and address areas of concern.

To be a great, supportive job development manager, you must:

1. Make sure you have enough job developers to place the number of clients that truly need job development.

2. Know what job development is and how it differs from order taking and job matching.

3. Communicate with job developers about job expectations and how they are performing against expectations.

4. Support job developers to implement strategies to engage employers.

5. Encourage and allow job developers to spend adequate time to focus on employer engagement activities. This includes reducing administrative and supply-focused work to enable more time communicating with employers by phone, email, and onsite follow-ups.

6. Troubleshoot with job developers to address such matters as team, employer, and client issues as they arise.

7. Evaluate employer engagement activities to determine if there is a return on investment. For

example, does the time spent on social media and schmoozing at networking events result in hidden market opportunities? Is the job developer able to convert job opportunities into job placements for clients with barriers to employment?

Job development success can be planned, measured, and resourced. Successful job developers can be hired, trained, and supported to be successful, and success requires discipline from employment service leaders, managers, and team members, including other job developers. Job development success directly impacts client success, and without successful job developers, some clients may never have the opportunity to go to work. Job development is complex and challenging, and it is also important, possible, and meaningful.

To deliver a service that leads to employment for all of your job seekers, you actually need to talk to employers (Dang!)—a lot of them, all of the time.

Imagine what you would be doing differently with your clients if you weren't teaching **them** to be job developers.

CONCLUSION:

Endnote by the Keynotes

CONCLUSION:

Endnote by the Keynotes

Ta-da!

Ta-da is usually a grand reveal that is kind of . . . positive. And it leaves the audience a bit mesmerized and in awe.

But in this book, *Smoke and Mirrors*, the big reveal is something that we all knew all along. It doesn't leave us in awe, or entertained, or smiling. It is exposure of deceit, cheating the system, systemic barriers, racism, sexism, ableism, etc. within program policy that encourages these practices.

The question is, how does it serve you?

How does continuing this practice serve you as politicians and public servants?

How does continuing this practice serve you as a service provider?

How does continuing this practice serve you as practitioners?

How does continuing this practice serve your clients and community?

We know how deeply uncomfortable partaking in the illusion is, and we also know you came to this field for purpose, not trickery.

Consider your sphere of influence. You can only change yourself, and this is your reality, so what are YOU going to do about it, within your sphere of influence?

As we said at the beginning, we are more optimistic than ever about the current direction of career and workforce development. Never before have we seen such interest in labour-market information and the future of work from so many players: government, employment-service providers, education, industry, academia, evaluators, and sector-specific associations and business consultants. No doubt, most of these players can see the reality of the situation and would like to be part of the solution. We'd like to be part of your solution too.

Let's begin, shall we?

ABOUT THE AUTHORS

SARAH AND ANGELA use a cheeky and humorous writing style to communicate the very serious issues at hand and show readers how they can stop being complicit in poor service delivery.

Together, Sarah and Angela bring a corporate memory that spans three decades of government-funded employment service programming and delivery, primarily in Canada. They have worked with numerous government departments and with thousands of management and front line staff working in hundreds of organizations.

With this book, it is the authors' hope that their readers will learn they have more power than they think they do to improve their services for marginalized populations.

Angela Hoyt (left) lives in Gananoque, Ontario, and Sarah Delicate (right) calls Bowmanville, Ontario home.